WHAT OTHERS ARE SAYING ABOUT ISAAC RUSSELL AND THIS BOOK

"The 'Success Model' of Isaac Russell's Success Plus is very unique. It is not a classroom instrumental environment. It is relationship-oriented through on-the-job interaction and mentoring. Think of it as coaching rather than training."

— John Sherman,
CEO, East Region,
Coca-Cola Bottling Company United, Inc.

"Experience tells me that Isaac Russell's Success Plus can establish a positive working attitude between top management and workers regarding productivity."

— George Howard,
Pioneer and Former Director,
Alabama Industrial Development Training

"Our company benefited from the services we received from Isaac. We feel they have improved communication and relationships with our employees."

— Allen Fletcher,
Former Administrator,
Northeast Alabama Regional Medical Center

"We have gained the respect of our employees through the training that was received for the managers/supervisors at our facility. This training gave us the insight that was needed for our managers/supervisors to understand the Leadership Competencies."

— Bob Massaro, Former
Human Resource Manager,
Tyson Foods

"Isaac was an amazing leadership coach who helped me take the development of my teams to a new level. After working with Isaac, I was able to develop systems and processes to drive improvement in myself and those who report to me. This led to improvement in all major metrics with my work teams, some of which improved more than 70 percent. The amazing part isn't the improvement; it's the sustainment in the improvements. With Isaac's help, I didn't just drive short-term change; I drove cultural change. The skills Isaac shared with me have changed how I manage people and will influence me for the rest of my career. I can't say enough about the training and development he shared with me!"

— Paul Novak,
Customer Satisfaction Manager,
Rockline Industries

"This book is an extremely practical guide for leadership. It is easy to just start running—especially when there is a burning platform and change is needed. But running doesn't mean you will win the race. You first need to understand the race route, who your competitors are, what the conditions are for the race, how the race will be measured, how to train properly, etc. In other words, you need a plan to win this race. That is exactly what this book is about. It will be your plan to win and boost your organization's bottom line."

— Mike Sutterer,
President,
Bonnie Plants, Inc.

"Isaac is a true friend and a fantastic resource! He works with you to help develop people, improve team dynamics and ultimately make you more money."

— Steve Jurek,
Former President,
GNP Company

"What can I say about this awesome man. Isaac and I have been friends for thirty-nine years. I have watched Isaac go from an hourly worker to a successful business owner. I believe his success comes from his faith in God and his ability to communicate with people of all ethnic, economic, and cultural backgrounds. Isaac's sense of humor, adventure, and life experiences have given him the ability to see any situation in a positive sense. Isaac's willingness to share his success with the people he loves is why he is an inspiration to me, my family, and many others."

— Abe Williams, Jr,
Longtime Friend

"The most challenging aspect of making a business thrive is optimizing the effectiveness of leaders and managers. That's where Isaac Russell of Success Plus Consulting comes in! Starting in the early 2000s, Isaac has provided expert consulting support to our managers and leadership teams in seafood production facilities in Alabama, Seattle, and Massachusetts. He helped transform work cultures during times of dynamic operational changes by partnering with frontline managers and providing one-on-one coaching on interpersonal effectiveness, managing business metrics, and developing collaborative leadership skills, among others. Isaac has a unique mentoring style that combines humor, often laced with fun Southern anecdotes, with pragmatic solution-oriented guidance gained through extensive experience in varied fields. He can relate effortlessly with CEOs and line workers alike. He meets people where he finds them and builds out from there—it's remarkable."

— Tammy French,
Former VP of Human Resources,
American Seafood Group

"Isaac's homespun wisdom is a breath of fresh air from the hundreds of business books flooding the market. He gets to the heart of the matter quickly and offers simple, practical, and realistic solutions to problems that seem overwhelming and complex. I am amazed by how well Isaac can educate and entertain at the same time. It's a rare gift."

— Cary Tutelman,
Family Business Consultant
and Author of *The Balance Point*

"After my first meeting with Isaac, I could tell immediately that he had the professionalism, poise, experience, and personality to move our company forward to achieve its objectives. As a new CEO, I was able to utilize Isaac to help me understand the culture of our organization and, just as importantly, determine if employees and leaders were 'getting' our messages about customer service, financial management, and leadership. Isaac did all that and more. The adjustments we made regarding defining expectations at all levels of our company led to immediate improvements. Isaac was also able to help our company identify—and remove—barriers to success. He's a friend, confidante, and mentor."

— Rick Lemonds,
President and CEO,
South Central Power

"I have seen Isaac Russell's Success Model at work first-hand, on-site within our company. It has positively impacted several first-line supervisors who have delivered higher-sustained KPIs and gone on to second and third promotions. Now you can read Isaac's book and continue your own journey of *Improving Profits Through People*."

— Cory Bouck,
Regional General Manager-Asia/Pacific,
Johnsonville Sausage

"I've long believed that the key to becoming an effective/good leader is directly tied to one's ability to develop genuine trust in relationships. Very early in his consulting role with our company, Isaac set about creating that reciprocal trust with each supervisor. When he hit roadblocks with some, he would discuss those challenges with me, but he never asked me to intervene. When I offered to help, he would respond with, 'Just give me a little more time; we'll find the common ground.' After three years of patience and perseverance, in a culture I don't believe Isaac was accustomed to, he did, in fact, 'find the common ground.' Able to build from the foundation of mutual trust, Isaac has sharpened the skills of our supervisory and management personnel to employ the principles of KPIs (Key Performance Indicators) to evaluate, measure, and improve our overall operation. Under Isaac's guidance, our team members have navigated a mindset shift. Our company and individual team members are poised for greater success as a direct result of Isaac's influence and leadership."

— Stan M. Cope,
Retired President,
Bonnie Plants, Inc.

"It has been a true joy to have worked with and witnessed Isaac's skills and methods in developing key leaders in my industry. He has an innate ability to peel away the root causes of ineffective leadership and replace the void with skills that energize the individual to perform. Over the years, I have been amazed by how Isaac has transformed some of our most seasoned leaders, motivating them to take that next real improvement step. Personally, he has truly helped me grow professionally, improving my performance in managing both down and up in my organization."

— Bill Petz,
Complex Manager,
Pilgrims WI Operations

"The practical leadership application of setting vision through driving results in the organization sounds simple in theory; however, it is difficult to hold in consistent practice in reality. Isaac's approach and cadence and his ability to fit that cadence within any operating system is valuable and it works—we can display this firsthand. The process connects a committed organization together and creates a consistent leadership approach that creates respect and integrity to all members of the organization while helping practice the true definition of accountability. This book is a must read for any level of leadership."

— Pat Rusch,
General Manager,
Rockline Industries

"This book covers Isaac Russell's teaching methods about investing time in your staff and holding people accountable at all levels of the organization. If you are not willing to make this investment of time, it will not work. You need to build some kind of relationship with your staff and they have to know you want to do that. Additionally, Isaac's book teaches management how to teach employees how to actually do their jobs, without doing it for them and while still keeping them accountable when they don't do it. Isaac shows how to make an investment in your staff because if you cannot get them to listen to you, they will never follow you. If you want to succeed in management, and improve profits through people, then start here!"

— Bobby Lecroy,
Manager at Trident Seafoods

"In *Improving Profits Through People*, Isaac Russell shares his years of experience helping businesses create their own destinies by helping their employees create theirs. Each chapter is filled with practical examples and exercises, personal experience in the trenches, and words of downhome wisdom. Isaac has a heart of gold, and the profits you will generate after you apply the principles in this book reflect that."

— Patrick Snow,
Publishing Coach and International Bestselling Author
of *Creating Your Own Destiny* and *The Affluent Entrepreneur*

"Isaac Russell's *Improving Profits Through People* puts aside all the business lingo to get to the heart of a business—its people. He focuses on the relationships between managers and employees, in both directions, teaching employees how to manage their managers and vice-versa. His humor gently points out foibles managers might make, and he teaches us all how to get along better in the workplace. I wish I had read this book years ago when I was a manager."

— Tyler R. Tichelaar,
PhD and Award-Winning Author of
Narrow Lives and *The Best Place*

LEADERSHIP IN A CHANGING WORLD

IMPROVING PROFITS THROUGH PEOPLE

BOOSTING YOUR ORGANIZATION'S BOTTOM LINE
WITH RESULTS-ORIENTED LEADERSHIP STRATEGIES

ISAAC RUSSELL

EXECUTIVE LEADERSHIP COACH

AVIVA
PUBLISHING
New York

IMPROVING PROFITS THROUGH PEOPLE
Boosting Your Organization's Bottom Line with Results-Oriented
Leadership Strategies

Published by:
Aviva Publishing
Lake Placid, NY
(518) 523-1320
www.AvivaPubs.com

Isaac Russell
256-453-5577
Isaac@SuccessPlusConsulting.com
www.SuccessPlusConsulting.com

ISBN: 978-1-63618-144-8

Library of Congress Control Number: 2021914713

Editor: Tyler Tichelaar, Superior Book Productions
Cover Design: Fusion Creative Works
Interior Book Layout: Fusion Creative Works

Every attempt has been made to properly source all quotes.

Printed in The United States of America

First Edition

2 4 6 8 10 12

DEDICATION

To my late wife, Valerie, raising kids from the ages of two and six by myself wasn't easy, but with the help of both of our families, sweetheart, I did it!

To my two children, Sheree and Carlson, may God be with you as you journey through this tough world.

To my mother, Daisy M. Russell, and my late father, Isaac Russell, Sr. You both instilled in me prayer, morals and values, and work ethic, which are life's foundation and have served me well throughout my life.

To my siblings, Denise, Edward, Negretta, Kevin, and Carol, thanks for being a close-knit family whose members get along very well and support one another. God bless you all.

To Steve Jurek, Devin Wood, Stan Cope, Brett Moreau, Rivers Myres, Dana Pressley, Mike Miller, Dave Fessenbecker, and Ratana Stephens, I have worked with lots of CEOs, presidents, and managers. You all stand out because you are not driven by status to impress others; you love people because you are comfortable in your own skin. You have hired and built relationships with people, no matter their gender, race, religion, or politics, and you didn't tolerate others who didn't in your organizations. Like my parents and me, you have standards and they weren't for sale. I commend and respect you for that.

To the late George Howard, you matched my God-given talent with the discipline of teaching and coaching others to be successful. You are greatly appreciated and missed.

To everyone I have worked with over the past thirty years, you've made me better, and I've shared your wisdom with others to make them better. My thanks to every company and the individuals I've coached.

ACKNOWLEDGMENTS

I would like to extend a special thank you to the following friends, associates, and those who helped me make this book possible:

Ken Andrews, Greg Auburt, Don Bennett, Patsy Bennett, David Bleth, Cory Bouck, Fynley Jane Bouck, Pam Brenny, Jane Brill, Rule Cowls, Mike Deramus, Alex DuPuis, Franklin Elston, Nathanial Elston, Keith Faulk, Arthur Fite, Ron Flathery, Glen Forbes, Stephanie Fowler, Tammy French, Susan Friedmann, Fred Gant, Sr., Rodney Gibson, Jarrod Goodman, Frank Hacker, Mike Helgeson, Todd Hobbs, Jeff Howard, Paul Howard, Denisa Hubbard, Randy Hubbard, Pat Hughes, GNP Company, David Israeli, Javarous Johnson, Sandi Jurek, Steve Jurek, Brian Klepke, Bill Lanners, Rick Lemonds, Charlie Lindsey, Scott Lyons, Scott Maddox, Bob Massaro, Eldo McCombs, Brett Moreau, Chris Morris, Rivers Myres, Nola, Laura Newman, Lenny Newman, Jarl O'Barr, Jodi Page, Mark Page, Bill Petz, Dana Presley, Anne Prior, Jeff Redmond, Russell Reeves, Toby Robin, Lamar Rotten, Charlie Rubio, Pat Rusch, The Russells, Kathleen Rydberg, Jack Sherman, John Sherman, Patrick Snow, Ratana Stephens, Steve Stoup, Mike Sutterer, Mike Tilley, The Swifts, The Teagues, The Whatleys, Tyler Tichelaar, Trident Seafoods, John Turner, Cary Tutelman, Cathy Tutelman, Gary Welch, Abe Williams, Chris Williams, Devin Wood, and Jae Wuori.

CONTENTS

SECTION 1: LEADERSHIP

SECTION 2: MOTIVATION

SECTION 3: PRODUCTIVITY

THE SUCCESS PLUS
TRAINING PHILOSOPHY

"Intellectual growth should commence at birth and cease only at death."

— Albert Einstein

"It is a thousand times better to have common sense without education than to have education without common sense."

— Isaac Russell

One of my favorite quotes I believe is applicable to the entire foundation of this book (and your workplace) is: "It is a thousand times better to have common sense without education than to have education without common sense." Most of this book is based on thirty-plus years of my experience working in manufacturing (from being on the production and service side all the way up to being the top leader, and everywhere in between). When making decisions within your organization that directly impact your profits, I encourage you to base your decisions on the proven principles summarized in this book.

I know how limited and valuable your time is, if you are like most busy, senior-ranking company officers, so I am honored that you are reading this book. If you do not have time to read it cover-to-cover and are looking for the Cliff Notes version or an executive summary, this Preface can be your saving grace. I dare you to read the philosophy here and begin to apply it to your organization. Better yet, delegate the reading of this book to your senior management team so positive change can occur.

I believe that:

Anyone with the physical and mental capabilities to do a job, who understands their job, and who has a clear understanding of what is expected of them, will do a good job.

When an employee doesn't perform, either they do not have the physical or mental capabilities, or they do not understand the job. Either way, it is your responsibility as management to assume you are not doing your job to help them and act accordingly.

Through testing, physical and mental abilities can be measured. The task then becomes to transform test-selected individuals into motivated and skilled employees. For effective training, a total involvement program is necessary. Not only is it imperative that the assigned management team of a given company provide specific information for the training program's development, but the program must be designed to reinforce the particular management policies to be used.

An integral part of this book and the Success Plus training philosophy showcased in it is to have each management member assume their proper role in the management-of-people process to develop positive attitudes through total involvement...with the end goal being to produce a quality product, through training, with maximum efficiency, in the minimum time.

Most organizations' major weakness lies in frontline supervision. To the average worker in the organization, their supervisor is "the company." The relationship between the frontline supervisor and their subordinates determines attitudes and motivation within the organization. However, in many cases, proper training of supervisory personnel is neglected. For this reason, my training and coaching stresses proper training of frontline supervisors and their integration into the management team.

Only after a management philosophy has been defined, and each member of the management team is well versed in this philosophy, can a useful training program be implemented.

Training's value to the company depends upon results, not complex ideas or individual philosophy. The primary task of any training program is to fill specific jobs with qualified people. The training process must be simple, and to prepare an individual for a particular job, the job must be well detailed and defined.

Each company has a unique product, and it is often a difficult product to manufacture. The skills required and used differ from company to company, and each company is unique in its management personality, methods, and techniques. For these reasons, management and training must work together to generate those skills and attitudes necessary to obtain maximum results. The training program is then designed to give the trainees the skills to do the job, and more importantly, to instill in them the primary requisites for doing any job well...proper attitudes, motivation, and pride in quality workmanship.

My goal for you, your team, and your organization is to succeed in achieving your desired profits while sharing the same vision and collaborating to get on the same page moving forward. Your challenge will be to align your leadership goals for the company with each of your departments. My hope is this book will convince you to create and execute a strategic plan while working together with your team and organization to eradicate and overcome all the obstacles that enter your path.

FIVE STEPS TO IMPROVING PROFITS THROUGH PEOPLE

In case you are not able to read the entire book, I have positioned upfront the five steps below so you can get the Cliff Notes version. If you are to turn a profit and get your people working in harmony as a team, these five things must occur in your organization:

1. **Vision:** How do you see yourself being successful? How do you see your team being successful? What are you willing to accomplish? What does success look like for just your department? The vision's purpose is to encourage leaders to talk to their subordinates not as a boss but as a business partner to share and compare their vision. Only after each person discusses the vision and is willing to collaborate on one vision can they discuss how to accomplish the vision. The subordinate is to follow the same pattern down to the hourly worker. Once the vision gets to the hourly worker or the frontline person closest to the customer or consumer who produces or sells the product, the vision can then transform into a job being done and very well defined.

2. **Goal:** What are you measuring for success to achieve your vision? How are you measuring? What are you willing to accomplish? The goal must match the vision; everyone must meet to align with that vision. (Repeat the process above with your subordinate and down to the person closest to the customer or the person who makes the product.)

3. **Plan:** I encourage you to have all leaders produce a written plan or plans to accomplish the vision and the goal. (Putting them in writing crystalizes the goal so it can become reality.) Most leaders enter their jobs without a plan, so they unintentionally plan to fail. Be sure to include your standards and leadership style and lead by example, define jobs, and make adjustments to the plans as needed. It's your job to instill these plans in all leaders for teaching down. Make sure to discuss plans with your leader, just as you discussed the vision and goal.

4. **Process:** The process is the start of the plans' execution and the managing of those plans by the leaders whose people built the plans. Management of the plans includes tracking the Key Performance Indicators (KPIs), company policies, and the company's leadership style. Things will go wrong in the process, so this step will test and gauge your teaching ability. Analyzing your process and business and making adjustments in real time will be vital, along with maintaining morale. What can go wrong will go wrong in the process. The process is a grind, but remember: "Repetition is the mother of all learning."

5. **Results:** How do you measure results from your goals, scorecard, or KPIs? This must be discussed in the goal

and planning stage by all leaders and frontline workers. What adjustments are we making when we fall short of the goals? What is the plan to educate or mentor? How are you identifying performers and non-performers? How are you gauging people's morale and keeping them positive?

The answer is to conduct one-on-ones because it is important to make sure people don't lose sight of the vision, goal, their particular plan, and the results, depending on the job that was defined. Make sure you make them think! In the one-on-one, you will review all of the steps and follow up.

Please refer to the Task Correction sheet in Appendix A. It is a tool to help educate and redefine a job that, in the process, went wrong from the plan. The true measure of success is not to let the fire recur once you put it out. Once you and the team have collaborated and are on the same page about the task's correction, that particular task correction goes on a focus list. (Once on the focus list, it doesn't come off, and it is checked routinely to make sure it doesn't recur during unscheduled one-on-ones with employees. A focus list can have upwards of ten to fifteen items, depending upon how detailed the teacher was in the process phase.)

CASE STUDIES USING THESE FIVE STEPS

Below are four case studies of real companies and real management teams that have applied these five steps to their processes, along with their real results:

Rockline Industries (Sheboygan, Wisconsin)

Pat Rusch, General Manager of Rockline Industries, and his staff have improved the bottom line by using parts of the five steps to improve efficiencies and productivity. They have used the focus list, the process, vision, and goal, along with Rockline's operating principles and KPIs. The staff also used the format for the one-on-ones to engage Rockline Associates on the production floor. This led to better retention and morale, thus adding savings to the bottom line. Rockline Industries sees the value of implementing the five steps or parts of the steps to perfect their company goals. Rockline sees the value in earning profits through their people by having a well-educated workforce. Most importantly, Rockline, as a company, understands that by educating their workforce, they are investing in their company.

Bonnie Plant Farm (Union Springs, Alabama)

Bonnie has improved its labor cost through being efficient by using KPIs and goals. They have done so by educating supervisors and managers on how to execute the vision, goals, and plan. They did this by listening to input from the leaders and employees who actually do the work. The change in employee mindset and habits has been exciting! Through leadership efforts, waste has turned into profits. The tray recovery department and other departments have saved money, thus improving profits through their people. The Bonnie leadership team of supervisors and managers has done a terrific job at growing into change.

Trident Seafoods (Carrollton, Georgia)

Brett Moreau, plant manager of Trident Seafoods, understands the five steps of profit through people. It's evident from his coaching, teaching, and mentoring as a leader. Teaching comes naturally to Brett. I am so proud of him; we worked together when he was a young leader, and he has developed into one of the best I've seen.

He can transform a non-performing organization into a performing one! And he loves it! Brett understands the value of frontline supervision and its integration into the workforce. If you don't understand your numbers, you don't understand your business. With that in mind, Brett believes in the continuous education of the frontline supervisor. The Trident Seafoods team in Carrollton, Georgia, has turned a non-performing plant into a performing plant. The greatest asset is having a plant manager who believes in frontline supervisor training and giving frontline supervisors the power to manage their processes based on KPIs.

GNP Company (St. Cloud, Minnesota)

Over the years, GNP Company (a poultry manufacturing company whose initials stand for Gold'n Plump) has been a model of using the five steps to success in part or in their entirety to improve the bottom line in all of its plants. Through using the steps, it has improved yield, turnover, waste, efficiency, and teamwork. Steve Jurek, president of GNP, understood the value of people, and he has had smart people working with him who fully supported the process and saw that it worked. The poultry business has one of the highest turnover rates of any industry, but GNP has controlled its turnover and can stand beside anyone in the industry. The leaders at GNP installed training programs and have always led the industry in innovation and education. The company's success reflects a true group effort by many people who have developed the right culture.

WHAT YOU WILL LEARN

The above is an executive summary of what you will learn in the pages ahead. We will further discuss the five steps for improving profits through people, and look more closely at the case studies of companies I have consulted with over the years. I hope you will enjoy the material and that this book will be the training resource you have been searching for to assist you in solving some of your greatest organizational challenges.

Remember, as a leader, you pay people to think, so let them! Stop being a control freak or everyone will shut down and stop thinking. Boom! There goes your future to lead. You can piss on the fire and call the dogs in then because "that hunt's over"! In other words, you won't have long-term success until all of your people are involved. So start teaching, coaching, and mentoring, and stop being a doer. Also, spend time around your processes and people so you can see things through their eyes.

Now, are you ready to dive more deeply into how to improve profits through people? Then let's begin. I hope you enjoy and benefit from this journey.

RE-TOOLING YOUR BUSINESS
MODEL WITH PEOPLE

"Give me a lever long enough and a fulcrum on which
to place it, and I shall move the world."

— Archimedes

"Most leaders are like sheep without a shepherd.
They can't stand to be alone, to make hard decisions,
or to overcome adversities."

— Isaac's Saying

It is 2 a.m. on a Tuesday. You are tossing and turning (yet again), agonizing over your responsibilities at work and suffering because your mind just won't shut down. You wonder just how in the world you are going to be successful when the alarm rings at 5 a.m. and you have wasted another night with no sleep!

Your mind just won't turn off as you continue to stress and worry about the safety of your employees, your production schedule, and what will happen if you miss your deadline. You are concerned about brand reputation, improving customer satisfaction, product recall, and the damage to your top leadership team should the worst actually happen. You are stressed about labor shortage, loss of products, and your ability to lead your organization through all these fires. If you fail, what will your board of directors think? You are concerned if your job is safe; you're worried about being let go!

Not only is your mind spinning from this never-ending laundry list of worries…but you are actually seeing all this stress and worry take a serious toll on your personal health. You can't sleep through the night, you have gained weight, you are suffering from a poor diet, and you have not been to the gym in who knows how long.

More importantly, your relationships are suffering, your spouse is concerned, and you are not there for your kids as much as you would like to be. You are asking yourself, "How long can I keep up this pace? Am I doomed to failure? Is a personal breakdown just around the corner?"

If you have experienced sleepless nights, emotional stress, and ongoing anxiety, I want you to know there is hope. There are solutions and strategies for you and your organization to implement to right your ship and achieve the organizational goals your shareholders and company owners have set for you and your organization.

In this book, you will learn how to improve your effectiveness through your people, and you will also learn why you should assume nothing and teach everything. As a result, your team will be prepared and trained to achieve all the organizational goals you are charged with achieving.

Furthermore, you will learn how to become the leader others *want* to follow. You will learn how to motivate your workforce to achieve Key Performance Indicators (KPIs). You will manage not only your work friends, or even your bosses, but all of your team to achieve common goals. Furthermore, you will learn how to hire selectively to combat labor shortages. You will learn how to survive and reverse loss of profits, and most importantly, how to nourish a safe work environment for your team so you can continuously keep employees motivated and earn profits.

I purposely made this book an easy read because I know you have lots on your plate and don't have time to dive into a complicated text. This book is not about science, algorithms, technology, automation, or profit and loss statements. It is about people, simply about people and how to engage them and treat them right. Some of the suggestions offered in this book seem quite obvious, but you would be amazed how many organizations I consult with do not treat their most valued assets (their employees) as human beings. This is an easy-to-follow book with lots of short chapters (and a few long ones) full of bite-sized nuggets of information.

What I offer in these pages is simple—overlooked management strategies to ensure success for your people and your organization. The brilliance of this book is it teaches you how to treat people with dignity and respect and get the most out of your people so they will help you achieve your organization's vision and goals so together you can achieve profits. Also, please note that profit is not a dirty word because it is where your raises and benefits come from. More profit and more growth means more opportunities for more people to get promoted and take on more responsibility. Most importantly, this book can and will serve as your manufacturing blueprint for "Leadership in a Changing World" (which also happens to be the title of my keynote speech).

If you apply the wisdom, knowledge, experience, skills, strategies, and techniques offered in these pages to your life, you will achieve what this book's title and subtitle promise: Boosting Your Organization's Bottom Line with a Results-Oriented Leadership Process. By using this process, you will literally improve profits through people, which is this book's goal. Additionally, you will get the bonus or promotion you desire, and it will come with a pretty solid increase in pay and a healthier mind.

So, why should you look to me to solve your organization's challenges? Because achieving these metrics for major companies all over the world has been my lifetime professional goal and practice. I founded Success Plus in 1993 to provide hands-on management training and coaching to companies worldwide in the industrial, manufacturing, customer service, and service industries. I have established myself as a leader in this field with thirty combined years as a manager and business owner. My main area of concentration for the last twenty years has been the industrial, manufacturing, customer service, and service arenas.

For more than thirty years, I have helped some of America's most recognized brands, such as Coca-Cola, Tyson Foods, and Johnsonville Sausage, increase productivity, reduce turnover, boost profits, and create stronger relationships between leadership teams and their employees. I credit much of my own success to my mentor, the late George Howard, the man who pioneered the leadership of Alabama, Georgia, South Carolina, and Florida's Industrial Development Training.

Consequently, I understand why your organization is not firing on all cylinders. I know being a respected leader is harder than those on the outside realize. I know you may be caring for aging parents, have a special needs child, or perhaps even some of your own health challenges. I want you to know it is okay to feel apprehensive about your ability to lead your organization to the next level. But knowing you are taking the time to read this book and apply its wisdom gives me confidence in your ability. I believe in you!

I will challenge you here, and throughout this book, as you learn how to best improve your profits through your people, to always remember:

ASSUME

NOTHING;

TEACH

EVERYTHING!

Because you have nothing to lose except people and profits! Moving forward, I want to be your leadership and productivity coach. I want to be your virtual mentor and accountability partner. I want to be the shoulder you can lean on during tough times. I want to be your friend, the person and resource you look toward to overcome your challenges so you can lead your company to record profits. I am very confident, and my track record has proven that I can help any business make money. I just need a willing soul who will provide me and my "Improving Profits" system with access to their organization. After reading this book, perhaps you will be that willing soul.

Are you ready to begin? Are you ready to step outside of your box? Are you ready to expand your comfort zone and step into the new person you are becoming? Are you ready to achieve your personal goals and your organization's goals? If so, let's get started and take this journey together! Now is your time! Let's go!

P.S. At the beginning of each chapter, I have included both a "business quote" and an "Isaac's Saying," both of which drive home that chapter's point. The first quote will help you understand the chapter's meaning. The second quote reflects who I am, so it may only register with you if you have spent some time with me. These are quotes I have learned over the years from my elders and friends. Either way, I hope you are entertained with these Southern quotes. Having grown up in Alabama, I wanted to share a bit of my culture with you in this way (mostly in terms of work ethic, but also in terms of our direct, slang-like communications). Either way, I am hopeful these wise quotes will give you some laughs, and more importantly, spur you on to think deeply and act differently.

Isaac Russell

SECTION 1

LEADERSHIP

"The key to becoming an effective leader is not to focus on making
other people follow, but on making yourself the
kind of person they want to follow."

— John C. Maxwell

"Some leaders can't lead a bunch of scouts out of a tent.
Stop focusing on yourself and focus on others."

— Isaac's Saying

CHAPTER 1

IMPLEMENTING
YOUR LEADERSHIP

"Good business leaders create a vision, articulate
the vision, passionately own the vision, and
relentlessly drive it to completion."

— Jack Welch

"Excuses only sound good to the people who make them."

— Isaac's Saying

John Maxwell and Jack Welch are both correct: The success of virtually every organization on the planet comes down to how effective the leadership team is at getting employees to buy into their vision, and the best way to do that is to get them to buy into the people implementing the vision. The challenge is that often employees are unclear about the organization's vision and mission, whom to follow, and who is in charge. In this chapter, I will share how to actually implement leadership within your organization. But first let me define "leadership" for you.

One of my major goals in this book is to share how to perform your leadership responsibility effectively so you can achieve the organizational results that the owner, your shareholders, and/or the board of directors aspire to achieve. The challenge is how to do this "effectively" since lots of people are successful at leading ineffectively. One of the biggest reasons people quit their jobs is they are quitting their bosses. To be effective as a leader, your leadership skills need to be so good that no one will ever want to quit on you. Achieving that kind of success is the goal of this book and, in particular, this chapter.

But before I dive into leadership styles, I want to share a bit about me and where I first learned about leadership. I have had good mentors, been around good leaders, and also learned what not to do from bad leaders. Also, I have learned about leadership, work ethic, communication, and many other things. I grew up in Alabama as the oldest of six kids; I was a proud son who yearned to do right by my parents. Both parents influenced me in ways that serve me well today, but my father's leadership and work ethic still shine brightly in my heart! Both taught me how to work and instilled in me morals and values. I saw my parents embrace and communicate with a variety of people before and after integration in the South. My father was a Korean War veteran; after the service, he came back to the States and soon graduated from college. He became a math and science teacher and then a principal. During the summers, my father displayed his leadership style and work ethic by working side jobs to earn extra money to provide for me and my five siblings. He operated a backhoe tractor, dug septic systems, and built rock walls. Eventually, he completely built our family home out of recycled materials he had collected over the years. My parents were very smart in wanting their children to benefit from the formal education system. My mother was the rock of the family, ensuring we all got what we needed and did what we should. My parents led by example. I am so very grateful that they taught me not to blame others for my setbacks but to overcome adversity and push forward. They each had their own leadership style, which is now ingrained into me.

I attended school in the South during the time when the schools were being integrated. This was quite an experience. I learned that all tears are the same, regardless of your skin color. My mentors, my father, George Howard, Jim Griffin, and too many others to mention taught me about taking the self-leadership role in your life and working for what you earn. Consequently, I have been working as long as I can remember. In high school, I bagged groceries and mopped floors. From there I got into manufacturing, then management, became a business owner, and then began leadership mentoring and consulting.

In high school, a girl named Valerie caught my attention, and so the chase began. I chased her for years until she finally gave in and became my wife. We were happily married until Valerie was killed in a car/train accident. Being left to raise two kids, ages two and six, you can imagine I was crushed. But there wasn't time to grieve since being a single dad, those two completely depended on me. Being the oldest of six siblings, I knew a thing or two about raising kids, so from that moment on, my full-time job was to protect, love, and lead my two children to adulthood. Everything worked out, and today, I am proud of my family. Adversity, hard work, and love have all taught me a thing or two about leadership.

Whether it be in leadership, love, or work, I have learned over the years that results depend on relationships. Consequently, I will always be grateful to my parents. I am also grateful for all those I have had the opportunity and pleasure to lead in my work life.

I have also learned the importance of setting goals, taking the leadership role in your life, and why both are so very important. For years, I have said, "The people who don't set goals in life will always work for the people who do."

Furthermore, I don't want you to think that leadership and learning how to implement your leadership style is just a means to an end to earn more money. It is not. Self-leadership and setting goals may boost your income, but true wealth is found in relationships, not in money. I would rather be a millionaire "in friends" than a "millionaire in money."

Keep all that in mind as you develop your leadership style.

WHAT IS LEADERSHIP?

Leadership is defined by the dictionary as "The action of leading a group of people or an organization" or "the state or position of being a leader." My definition is "Leadership is an art." It is "the art of getting things done through people." This is an age-old definition full of meaning. As a leader, you are often a manager. Hence, management is an art because much like an artist, the manager creates order out of disorder. They achieve that order through vision, craft, and a means of communication, just like an artist does. Much of what a manager does consists of the intangible and complex dynamics of human relationships. It takes artistry to interact with people and get results from them.

Leadership is getting things done. Period. This means things will be done efficiently and done right. It also means doing the "right things" to be effective. By right things, I mean worthy objectives, relevant standards, and measurable results.

Additionally, leadership is getting things done "through people." That means it is your job to supervise the performance of subordinates in carrying out their responsibilities. Your major achievement will largely be effected in their collaborative achievement. Your subordinates understand what needs to be done, accept it willingly, and commit to it enthusiastically. In addition to getting results from supervising, you also achieve results by interacting with others: your boss, peers, staff, customers, etc. The message is clear—to be successful as a leader, you must engage the cooperation of others to achieve the right things in the most effective and efficient manner.

Finally, leadership is a process. Like management, leadership involves doing something that requires a number of steps. Leadership is a process of planning, organizing, coordinating, directing, and controlling the directions of work to achieve an objective. I will talk about each of these definitions in more detail later in the book, but first, let's dive into leadership philosophy and leadership style.

IMPLEMENTING ONE LEADERSHIP PHILOSOPHY AND ONE LEADERSHIP STYLE

Any successful organization can only have one philosophy and one style of leadership. This one philosophy needs to be practiced on a daily basis by everyone in senior leadership. I consult for organizations all over North America, and in the process, I often help them adopt the philosophy that one must lead by example and there can be no favorites. This philosophy, in my experience, needs to be based on three success principles:

1. **Listen:** As the leader, you must listen to the other leaders in your organization, your employees, and your customers.

Gather feedback and use it to help you make critical decisions to serve everyone involved, provided the decisions positively move the business forward from a moral and business standpoint. Follow-up is of the utmost importance.

2. **Lead:** An organization and its leaders lead by providing a consistent quality product in a consistent manner that focuses on achieving excellence. Excellence is achieved through continuous improvement both in performance and product innovation.

3. **Thrive:** You can ensure your organization thrives by balancing your business' needs with those of your people, your partners, the community, and the planet. We can thrive through how we engage our people, treat our people, and expect our people to treat each other, while establishing boundaries to ensure discipline is maintained. Ultimately, we want to produce a collaborative workspace that ensures no one is disrespectful to anyone else.

When you follow this three-step process of implementing one leadership philosophy, all your employees will be on the same page and working toward achieving the same results. When done correctly, everyone wins and everything runs efficiently.

COMMUNICATING EXPECTATIONS

One challenge all leaders have, and I am sure you have experienced, is knowing what you expect from your team and what your team expects from you. Often, your team is unclear about what is expected of them; as a result, the productivity target may be missed. Consequently, I communicate the following to all of the organizations I mentor so everyone can be on the same page.

Anyone who has the physical and mental capabilities to do a job and understands what is expected of them will do a good job. When your team member does not perform, either they do not have the physical or mental capabilities to perform, or they do not understand the job. Either way, you and your leadership team should assume you are not doing your jobs and act accordingly.

The best way to act accordingly is to properly communicate everything that is expected of them and the desired results. The best way to communicate with your team is to:

1. Meet and greet your team members daily. (If you speak with one, you have to speak with them all.)

2. Keep your door open to team members and encourage them to drop in often. (If you listen and follow up, you won't have to encourage.)

3. Listen as much as you talk. (Be a facilitator, not a boss.)

4. Give (and receive) feedback on a frequent basis. (Follow up.)

5. Communicate tasks clearly and avoid misunderstandings. (Eliminate gray areas.)

6. Explain "why" as often as needed. (People buy reasons why they do things.)

7. Assume nothing and teach everything. (I mean everything.)

When you follow this protocol, you will be amazed by how much smoother things will run in your organization. Also, you will be better able to communicate and help your employees understand how to evolve from setting goals to achieving results. They will be able to apply this understanding not only at work but in their personal lives—it's something they can share with their families to make everyone's lives better.

UNDERSTANDING THE VISION

As a leader, you are under tremendous pressure to clearly articulate the vision and the goals to your team so they can clearly understand and support them. The best way to do this is to follow these steps:

1. Communicate the Vision to your team.

2. Set team Goals to support that vision.

3. Put a Plan in place that will help make the vision and goals achievable.

4. Follow the Process that will support the plan.

5. Allow the process to deliver the desired organizational Results.

Communicating and implementing these five steps is extremely important if you are to effectively lead your team to support your company's desired profit and goals. The better you become at leading your team through this process, the more success your team will have, and the more you will find yourself in a position to be promoted and earn pay raises (both of which are important for you, I hope). Or if you are happy where you are, perhaps you will just want to be good at what you do. (I understand that too.)

PUTTING THE GOALS IN PLACE

Once one leadership style and one philosophy have been communicated and the proper communication method used so everyone is on the same page, the goals can be set, executed, and achieved. However, because everyone does not have the same level of training or experience, the organization's goals will only be realized if all team members can receive the same training so they can all execute toward the same vision. Therefore, one training methodology must be used to get everyone on board to build toward achieving the same goals. Team members on the same production page can ultimately work together toward achieving all the production goals set forth by management.

Your leadership style and philosophy should be based on three things: Key Performance Indicators (which I will discuss in full later in Chapter 17), company policy, and goals; the last may come to look different as you move down the leadership chain. For example, at the top, a vision means "What does success look like in our organization, and do we all have the same vision of what it looks like?" The vision is not a mission statement; it's a mental state and focus to drive success, but it's important for everyone to be on the same page about what drives success and revenue to improve the profits. What are the goals that have to be achieved to make the vision a reality? Those two will vary from top to bottom and have to be taught.

EXERCISE

List three ways you will effectively implement your leadership style that reflect listening, leading, and thriving.

_____

_____

_____

_____

_____

_____

_____

_____

_____

SUMMARY

The bottom line is that leadership development is needed, but it doesn't always happen correctly. Leadership development has to be intentional, focused, and ongoing. When done correctly—through implementation of one style with effective communication and clear expectations, understanding the vision, and finally putting it all together with everyone pursuing the same goals—magic happens. On the next page is the formula that should be the hallmark for implementing your leadership and ultimately getting closer to achieving your organization's revenue goals:

Knowledge

+

Skills

+

Ability

=

Productivity

Knowledge: Be a subject expert. Do your homework, and know the right questions to ask.

Skills: Communication skills are a must for bringing a team together on the same page.

Ability: You must have the physical and mental capability to learn to lead.

Productivity: Your productivity, or lack of, defines who you are as a leader.

CHAPTER 2

UNDERSTANDING HOW
GOOD LEADERS THINK

"The world as we have created it is the process of our thinking.
It cannot be changed without changing our thinking."

— Albert Einstein

"One person who thinks is more dangerous
than a thousand who don't."

— Isaac's Saying

In the last chapter, we discussed how to implement a common leadership style that supports the organization's visions, values, and goals. In this chapter, I will share how good leaders think and why thinking is so important for you as a leader. But first, I want to take a deeper look at what Napoleon Hill said about thinking: "The most important trait for success in business is the act of accurate thinking." This chapter will help you think better, build a core team, and get everyone on the same page. These processes are crucial for achieving your organizational goals.

Before we dive in, let me share a little about a man who had thinking like no other. Jim Griffin was my neighbor when I was a kid, but he became a mentor. Often when I wasn't doing chores or working with my father, I worked with Mr. Jim. After school or on weekends, we would demolish old houses—just the two of us! He was well into his sixties and I was just a teen. We also drove around town in a truck, delivering coal to customers with wood-burning stoves. We would talk about the value of a dollar, the value of working, and the value of staying out of trouble. These conversations gave me a first-hand account of how one amazing man lived his life and offered me insights on how I could live mine. I learned more from Mr. Jim than I did from any book, even though he was not a man educated in any formal education system. Mr. Jim always said, "It's a thousand times better to have common sense without education than to have an education without common sense." He was well respected in our community, and I was blessed to learn how his thinking could completely change the trajectory of a young man's life. He didn't have much, but he had enough. Mr. Jim was a good mentor and coach! I will be forever thankful for the time we spent together and what I learned from him about how good leaders think.

THE MIND OF GREAT LEADERS

When you look at how to effectively build and lead an organization to achieve major company goals, you must ask and consider the following:

- What is the process flow?

- How do I get clear communication between workers, managers, and executives about the goal?

- What constitutes safety for all the workers and how do I communicate how to practice safety?

- How do I get buy-in of the vision, goal, and plan?

- What constitutes and promotes quality in our manufactured product and brand?

- What constitutes quality in the customer service experience?

As a leader, you must think about, act on, and implement these things. You must also have a clear heart free of all prejudices, including race, gender, religion, and disabilities. This lack of prejudice is extremely important if all your team members are to follow your vision. This mindset must be your major focus so your team can focus on the goals you and the organization place before your team.

As a leader, you must be respectful and love to be part of someone else's success, to see them smile with tears of joy. You must strongly believe you can get a variety of personalities together and influence those personalities with the enthusiasm to achieve a goal while putting the team first. You must strongly believe you can challenge your team to the fullest while still letting them know how much you care about them and their success. As a leader, that's the way you must think. As a leader, you must think you have a career, an obligation, a calling, and not a job. If this position is just a pay raise and a power grab, it really is just a job and you are not truly a leader.

I challenge you to step up and do this leadership thing! It is your gift! It is your calling! You can be the leader people will follow because they "want to," not because they "have to." Have the mindset of believing in and caring about others so they can become empowered to achieve their goals through the organization's success. This is the vision and mindset you must develop as a true leader.

My friend, Charlie Lindsey, once gave me the following poem by Walter D. Wintle that describes for me true leadership:

Thinking

If you think you are beaten, you are;
If you think you dare not, you don't.
If you'd like to win, but you think you can't,
It is almost a cinch you won't.

If you think you'll lose, you've lost;
For out in this world we find
Success begins with a person's will
It's all in the state of mind.

If you think you're outclassed, you are;
You've got to think high to rise.
You've got to be sure of yourself before
You can ever win the prize.

Life's battles don't always go
To the stronger or faster man;
But sooner or later the person who wins
Is the one who thinks he can!

This is the type of thinking and mindset I challenge you to adopt as the leader! If you don't have it, you can't instill it in your people because you must lead by example.

BUILDING YOUR CORE TEAM

To be successful as a leader, it is vitally important to build a team. To do so, you must understand that you have to mesh people's personalities together to form a team. This process can be quite challenging because you may have to deal with conflicting personalities daily while staying in a positive mindset to pursue goals and implement company policies.

To build your team successfully, answer the following questions for yourself:

How do I get my team to understand the big picture?
(Meaning can they understand where they fit in?)

How do I explain how important their jobs are to me, and the goal?
(You can't do it alone, so build relationships.)

How can I influence them to understand how important they are to each other and why?
(Understanding this establishes the culture.)

How do I motivate them daily?
(Make them feel important and respected; show that you care.)

How do I motivate myself daily?
(Pray and hang around positive people because they never quit.)

How do I get each person and process to improve?
(Inspect what you expect by using testing methods and being a subject matter expert.)

Am I the only person who can see the vision, goal, and plan?
(You will learn this in the process phase of the five steps stated in the preface.)

Am I the only person who can analyze the process?
(Your scorecard will be the answer; then teach accordingly.)

Am I the only person who can see things that will happen before they happen?

(It depends on how well you can teach your leaders and how well they can develop their people.)

As you build the core of your team, ask yourself these questions. When you are looking for and interviewing talent, do all you can to find and hire people who have more talent and stronger skill sets than you have. When you do this, your core team will be in a great position to make your leadership role more rewarding. That's how I think because I know if I want to be successful, I cannot do it alone. As a leader, my challenge to you is to think in a similar way.

EDUCATING EVERYONE TO GET ON THE SAME PAGE

Fellow Southerner, best-selling author, and arguably one of the best speakers of our time, Zig Ziglar, has said for years: "You can have everything in life you want, if you will just help other people get what they want."

When you put your team's needs ahead of your needs, when you find out what their needs are, and then help them achieve them, they will go out of their way to achieve any task, goal, deadline, or vision you have communicated to them. What they want is to be respected, involved, and a part of something. As a leader you pay people to think, so stop being a boss and become an educator, teacher, motivator, and goal setter who inspires others to do the thinking.

EXERCISE

List three ways that, as the leader of your organization, you will begin to think differently.

_____

_____

_____

SUMMARY

To succeed in leadership, you must know how to think like a leader. The best leaders build amazing teams, and you must do the same because you can't achieve the organization's goals and higher profits by yourself. The best way to build great teams is through proper communication and education, and by making sure everyone is on the same page. When you do this, you are setting yourself and your organization up for massive success. When you educate your employees, you invest in your company. I challenge you to think this way.

CHAPTER 3

IMPLEMENTING YOUR CULTURE

"A culture of discipline is not a principle of business;
it is a principle of greatness."

— Jim Collins

"People will do what their culture allows."

— Isaac's Saying

In the last chapter, I shared strategies to help leaders think more clearly, build a core team, and get everyone on the same page. In this chapter, I will offer you strategies to help implement a culture of quality, consistency, and respect so there is no confusion about what is acceptable and what is not. This clarification will pay large dividends and help everyone get along in the spirit of harmony. Let's begin by defining culture.

WHAT IS CULTURE?

Culture is when a company defines the boundaries and discipline for running the organization from the top to the bottom to ensure success of the standard operating procedure. There can be only one leadership style and one philosophy in any culture. The Standard Operating Procedure (SOP) is followed at all times while educating the workforce on that culture and the importance of their role in the organization's success and culture. The culture should also communicate the message to all employees that they are respected and valued. Your people and your conversations with them are the foundation of the culture.

COMMUNICATING CORPORATE PHILOSOPHY

It is the senior leadership's responsibility not only to communicate the philosophy it stands for and wants it employees to operate by (thereby creating a company culture), but to lead by example before holding others accountable for not living up to the philosophy. Too many companies "talk the talk" but don't "walk the walk" when it comes to safety, culture, mission statements, etc. An organization can get better, or it can get worse, but it can't stay the same. The goal should be to always get better, and one of the best ways to do that is constantly to communicate the culture it is trying to build moving forward. The culture is the answer to your turnover problems, production problems, and customer service problems. If those problems are not resolved, they will lead to other problems that can result in loss of profits, more spending, and low employee morale, which will affect the organization at all levels.

FOUR WAYS TO IMPROVE YOUR COMPANY CULTURE

Company culture is perhaps the number-one factor for long-term success. Not only does it play a huge role in motivation and productivity, but it greatly affects turnover rates. In fact, workplaces with a strong, positive culture have voluntary turnover rates as low as 35 percent that of their peers or competitors.

Here are four simple ways you can start improving your culture today.

1. **Transparency:** When you run a transparent business, you create a culture where everyone is open and accountable for both daily operations and the business' future. When you allow employees to "see under the hood," they will not only have a better understanding of how the business works, but they will feel more invested in its success and give input.

2. **Diversity:** Diversity increases economic growth, provides valuable insights from multiple different viewpoints, and opens your business up to a greater share of the consumer market. More importantly, it increases respect and understanding among your workforce for different backgrounds, religions, races, genders, and sexual identities, which all make up the demographics of your customers and could affect your brand.

3. **Trust:** Trust goes hand-in-hand with transparency because to be transparent, you have to trust your employees. When you trust your employees to handle important tasks on their own, it builds confidence, increases productivity, and gives them a sense of purpose and belonging. You build trust based on what you teach. If you cannot teach, you cannot trust and motivate your employees, so knowing how to teach and coach is important.

4. **Communication:** A strong culture is an efficient culture, and you can't have either without communication. Give honest feedback and constructive criticism. Celebrate

wins. Dole out deserved compliments. More importantly, provide an open channel of communication between you and your employees. When employees feel they can come to you with any issue or idea, it will strengthen the overall relationship and create an all-around better culture.

CONSISTENCY WITH CULTURE

One way to achieve consistency as a leader once you have been promoted is to keep your hand out of your old job and let your replacement grow into their new responsibility. You need to be a leader, not a blamer or doer. Let your team members be the doers, and you be the leader and facilitator because that is how you achieve consistency. Let people know you believe in them; then lead by example, and stop being "the boss" aka "dumb ass" (meaning you have to tell people what to do all day and every day, with a negative attitude to boot). When you talk about your employees behind their backs, you will soon experience high turnover and low morale, which lead to low productivity and lost profits.

If you act this way, you are a dumb ass because that is what your employees are calling you behind your back (along with a few other choice words). I am calling you out to your face here because if you act like this, you are a non-leader in a leadership role. That kind of behavior has an effect on everyone's livelihood and it leads to an inconsistent and negative culture, the opposite of what you want.

TREATING ALL WITH RESPECT

Every leader's challenge is to try to influence highly intelligent humans to pursue a set of goals and visions that perhaps they did not set. The best way to get their buy-in is to respect them, engage them, and have them take ownership of the goal and vision. Give them a vested interest, and teach them everything you can without finger-pointing. You need to know (and I will say this over and over throughout this book) that you do not own people who work with you! They work for the organization, and your role is simply to facilitate their efforts in support of the company's goals and visions. When you explain everything in terms of why it is in their best interest, they will respect you and go the extra mile to achieve the goals at hand.

DEALING WITH INTERNAL CRISES

Crises happen. They are part of every company's culture. How you and your higher-ups handle crises will make or break your subordinates. You must have your standards and make every decision based on those standards. You must act and live your life at work according to the mission statement and company standards. When you operate from that perspective, your team will respect and partner with you to help you get through any crisis the organization faces. Frontline leaders are very important when dealing with a crisis because they are the closest to the workforce. Consequently, they must be very well trained in crisis management.

EXERCISE

Write 2-3 sentences about the culture you aspire to create among your team.

_____

_____

_____

_____

_____

_____

_____

_____

_____

_____

_____

_____

_____

SUMMARY

When implementing culture within your organization, you must begin with respect: respect for your employees, respect for your customers, and respect for the process. Culture doesn't automatically happen within the organization based on rules and policies; rather, it happens based on the actions of those running the company. If culture is to be effective, you must not so much be judged by what you say, but rather by what you do as the leader. Allow your actions to live up to a higher standard; then your subordinates will buy into your culture. Don't tolerate those who don't buy in because that will not only send an inconsistent message, but also harm the culture because you are disobeying your own standards. Remember, when you set the rules, people will watch you to see if you are the first to break them.

CHAPTER 4

BUILDING YOUR TEAM
AND KNOWING WHY

"If you want to lift yourself up, lift up someone else."

— Booker T. Washington

"People don't buy the 'what.' They buy the 'why'!"

— Isaac's Saying

In the last chapter, I defined culture and why it is important for all employees to understand it for the organization to run like a finely tuned engine. In this chapter, I will offer several ways to build your team, train your managers, and help all employees learn what they are doing, and more importantly, "why" they are doing it to support the organization's growth.

BUILDING AND RECRUITING YOUR CORE TEAM

When building your team, you must understand that "need" is a poor evaluator for talent. You need to look at your current roster of employees and ask yourself if you need to reduce it, add to it, or improve it in any way. You have to be willing to field questions from your employees based on their perceptions of what they need to better support their vision and goals.

When interviewing potential leadership candidates, I like to ask these questions:

1. Are you teachable? How do you feel about teaching others? Are you a teacher?

2. Have you worked in a system before? If so, explain how the system works and your part in it.

3. Do you know how to follow a plan? Do you know how to create a plan? Give me an example.

4. Are you more of a doer or a facilitator? Explain the difference.

5. Have you followed a mentorship trainee program? If so, explain the program.

6. How are your communication skills in terms of building a team and getting the team members to work together?

7. Have you ever been confined within the boundaries of a system?

8. If yes, how did you feel, and what were the results?

9. Are you willing to learn a new system and process?

10. Do you have humility when working with others?

When looking to hire employees or promote subordinates who have worked for you and the organization for several years, it is important to ask the interviewee what they would do differently or how they would change things. This is a very important question to internal candidates, so give them the opportunity to answer that question.

If you see strategy displayed in their answers, that strategy may be a sign they are a sure fit for the position. If, during the interview process, you identify a pattern among the interviewees that works for you and your process, feel free to hire accordingly to maintain the momentum. Always remember, communication skills are vital to success.

Also, remember when interviewing internal candidates that a large part of the interview will be based on their success as leaders; don't just look at references but consult their scorecard of success in leading a team. You will find they are stronger in some areas than others, but communication, goal setting, motivation, and teaching skills are a must. Once you become their leader, help mentor them, especially in their areas of weakness. Do your teaching and mentoring early in the process and connect it to goals or KPIs. Also know when to pull back and let them do their job. Don't hire leaders just because they do a job really well; being able to do doesn't mean they can lead. Do your homework; don't hire someone because of their experience with the company or because they are the last person standing because of turnover. Remember: "Need is a poor evaluator for talent."

TRAINING YOUR FRONTLINE LEADERS

Your job as the leader is to force change, and the only—and best—way to achieve change is through training. It all comes down to educating. So, here are some ways to be effective in training your frontline leaders.

Understand first and foremost that two-way communication is the key. Look for teaching skills in your leaders, but also look for their ability to develop relationships with their subordinates should they be placed in leadership positions. Your goal is to develop people at all levels who are both passionate and results-oriented. Every business is a result-based business.

When training, you can take all the previous ten questions and break them down into a lesson plan. In doing so, your goal is to eliminate all the reasons people will not perform for you. One way to get them to perform, as previously stated, is to treat everyone the same, regardless of sex, race, or education; eliminate stereotypes and show them that you genuinely care about their success and wellbeing.

KNOW WHAT YOU ARE DOING AND WHY

Remember my quote above: "People don't buy the 'what.' They buy the 'why'!" Understanding this fact is so important when it comes to training your team. When your employees are crystal clear about the why, they will do the right thing and go the extra mile to serve the customer (both the internal and external one).

Three examples of crystal-clear, well-taught training programs are those of Disney, Chick-Fil-A, and Waffle House. Service from these organizations is always a high-level, enjoyable experience. You can tell the workers are a team, all accepting their own roles and doing whatever it takes to serve the client to make it a memorable experience. Consistency is the word that describes the customer experience when visiting them. These companies have the same type of people you have. They just have better training programs because those programs are intentionally followed and ongoing.

These companies' training programs are about as good as it gets. You also need to do everything in your power to train your team to give this type of experience. When your people know the "why" behind what they are doing, your products and services will reflect this quality. Then you will develop a much better culture and a higher quality product or service.

EXERCISE

Write three strategies you will execute to build an even better team. Make sure you define what constitutes a better team and how to measure the results.

_____

_____

_____

SUMMARY

When you build your team and fully understand why you are building it, it should lead to profits for the organization, excellent service for your customer, and most importantly, a safe environment for your employees. As your organization hires more people, it is easy to assume labor is your biggest cost, but that is not the case. Your biggest cost is inefficient labor, but inefficient labor can only exist if inefficient leadership and training exist. Hence, your role as a leader is to build your team based on efficiency, relationships, and productivity, and the only way to do that is to "assume nothing and teach everything"!

CHAPTER 5

LEARNING WHAT
A PROCESS IS

"The work of art is above all a process."

— Paul Klee

"The process is a grind. What can go wrong
will go wrong in the process."

— Isaac's Saying

In the last chapter, I discussed the process of building your team and communicating to all employees the "why" behind all organizational objectives. In this chapter, I will introduce "process" into this mix (in terms of leadership as an art), and share why it is vital for the employees to buy into following a process in order to improve profits.

THE LEADERSHIP PROCESS EXPLAINED

No task can be efficiently accomplished unless it is wisely planned, properly organized, smoothly coordinated, understandably directed, and effectively controlled. These five broad functions of management are not separate and distinct, nor meant to be accomplished in a prescribed order. Instead, they are very much interrelated. At any one instance, perhaps all five are being applied simultaneously. What does this all mean? It means there are five functions of management, and as a manager, it is important for you to know all five as effectively as possible and understand when you are using them.

THE FIVE FUNCTIONS (AND QUESTIONS) OF MANAGEMENT

1. **Planning:** Planning is determining "what" is to be done, "where" it is to be done, "who" is responsible for doing it or seeing that it is done, "when" it is to be done, and sometimes "how" it is to be done. (Example: What are you aiming for and why?)

2. **Organizing:** Organizing is providing structure that establishes relationships between people and material grouped together for a common purpose. (Example: Who is involved and how?)

3. **Coordinating:** Coordinating is integrating all details necessary to accomplish the mission. (Example: Who keeps you informed and about what?)

4. **Directing:** Directing is issuing the necessary direction and instructions to subordinates and others to indicate what is to be done—the vital step between preparation and the actual operation. (Example: Who makes which decisions and when?)

5. **Controlling:** Controlling is acting to ensure that the plan actually comes together on time and within budget and the main objective is achieved. (Example: Who judges results and by what standards?)

EXECUTING THE PROCESS

Ultimately, the successful and competent supervisor (leader) uses the artistry of leadership to get results from others and, at the same time, employs the discipline of the process to manage the work. The process was created from the vision, goal, and plan. The process is how we get the results.

GRINDING YOUR WAY TO SUCCESS

As your team's leader, you are responsible for making certain your team helps turn a profit for your organization. To fulfill that responsibility, you will have to hire the right people to help you "grind your way to success"! Obviously, this is not your first rodeo, so you need to identify the truth, your truth, the standards, and the KPIs, and you must properly identify any and all areas in which your team is being prevented from turning a profit and creating a positive work environment. We have to compete to survive.

Then teach your plan to your team. Get them all on the same page in understanding what success is and is not. When you communicate the plan to your team, this core vision becomes the end goal. And if you are not about making profits, producing a quality product, and customer service, then you may need to have a gut check and ask yourself if you are the right leader for your team. This is what it means to grind your way to success (because everything in the vision, goal, and plan will be tested and adjusted in the process).

CLEARING THE PROBLEM AND GETTING BACK TO WORK

Sometimes, your team will get frustrated and believe that the process that either you or top management has put into place is the wrong process. This happens quite often in the manufacturing world when customer service, the workforce, or anyone involved in the process wasn't involved in the planning, so everyone is not on the same page. How do you overcome such roadblocks to your process?

Many companies will create meetings and put a team in place to try to solve the issue. The problem with that is whoever is assigned to this team may or may not have the management skill set, technology know-how, or ability to find a solution to the problem. We are then left wondering why the problem can't be fixed in minutes or hours and has to become a three-week meeting because we are thinking to find the answer by using everyone's tools. Instead, you have to stop and think: Do I have the wrong leader in that department or location?

When this happens, your team may experience what I call "paralysis by analysis." Then a major bottleneck will happen that affects your productivity. A leader should know their process, analyze it, and solve the problems before they become bigger problems. If you don't know your process, then you are in paralysis. You need to see what things could happen before they happen; otherwise, you may have to wait for your doer boss to bail you out with a project team that uses custom-fit tools in an off-the-rack world, only to still be unable to analyze your problem.

Do you see this happening with your team? As the leader, you need to nip this situation in the bud before these focus groups start analyzing you and your team. Instead step up, roll up your sleeves, and encourage everyone on your team to do the same. Then solve the problems and the issue internally through harder, more focused work. When you do this, you will succeed at avoiding a bunch of unwanted attention from your peers who may question your leadership ability. In the process, focus on achieving your Key Performance Indicators and your problem will be solved! If you have fifty employees, you have fifty consultants; they are the experts. To bring in others outside of your department to solve simple things is a slap in the face to your people. Don't do it unless it's absolutely necessary.

People on the frontline want to know you have walked in their shoes and you understand the language before they work with you. If so, they will give you the respect needed to change and deliver the results.

PUTTING ON WORK CLOTHES

Often, you and your team may be frustrated by the process; serious work then needs to be done to get past this. One reason for the frustration is somewhere along the line, your organization's process may be inefficient. Or perhaps the wrong team members are assigned to the wrong tasks. When this frustration occurs, you need to step up, put your work clothes on, and have one-on-ones (I'll teach you how to do that in Chapter 21) to find out what loose ends need to be resolved. Mentor, teach, coach, get more involved, and ask people their thoughts on the problem. Don't give them the answer until you challenge them to think. Encourage them to solve their own problems.

When frustrations set in, ineffective bosses may take it out on their team. Then turnover and absenteeism occur. While the lack of a system is at fault, doers may be tempted to believe this frustration is the root cause and that absenteeism and turnover reflect that their team doesn't like to work. The reality may be that they just don't like you. As a leader, you need to be fair, treat everyone the same, and attack the problems before they get out of hand. Frustrations and complaints from your staff are opportunities, so always view them as such. When things go wrong, your job is to create order out of disorder. Always remember to point the finger at the problems and not the people.

Perhaps the issue is your team is not fully trained. We will discuss that possibility in the next chapter. For now, you need to know that training takes time and is ongoing. People will get better based on what you teach, and the process will expose your teaching skills.

Also, consider that maybe the issue is not the process. Maybe the frustrations result from hiring the wrong people. When your team comes to meetings and brings their intellectual experiences or tools with them, make sure you are not the smartest person in the room. Henry Ford was so successful because he hired employees who were smarter and had more talent than he had; you need to do the same. But know the right questions to ask and be a subject matter expert. Also know there is no guarantee you can do the job better than the people doing it.

If you and your team fail, all the organization fails. Because failure happens system-wide, we just can't repeat our failures. It comes down to two types of people: doers and leaders. Your role as a leader is not to be the doer but the delegator. Delegate the doing task to your team so they can plan and think about how to become successful in the process so they can achieve the results from the vision, goal, and plan they created and bought into.

So, your challenge is to continue to put on your work clothes daily, and allow the doers to do while you and the other leaders lead. Communicate the plan so everyone is on the same page to ensure the process runs smoothly. Eradicate any roadblocks and move on.

EXERCISE

Write three new processes you will add to increase your team or division's productivity. Make sure they move the bottom line.

_____

_____

_____

_____

_____

_____

SUMMARY

As your team's leader, you need to manage the process so things will go smoothly. The best way to do this is to communicate with your team the importance of management to lead by using the five functions of: planning, organizing, coordinating, directing, and controlling. Then make sure you eliminate all problems through proper communication and execution. Remember, people are watching you in the heat of the battle, so stay calm. Frustration is an opportunity to teach and coach on KPIs, company policies, and leadership style.

Once everyone is crystal clear on their responsibilities, let the doers do and the leaders lead! When this happens harmoniously, you will have an effective team and boost profits. Keep your fingers out of everybody's pie and let them do their jobs. Be a leader and develop talent. Learn to teach. The process will become a mess if you don't. Remember, people will get better based on what's being taught.

CHAPTER 6

KNOWING ABOUT TEACHING, COACHING, AND MENTORING

"Education is the most powerful weapon which you can use to change the world."

— Nelson Mandela

"Nothing turns me off worse than a person who doesn't do their homework."

— Isaac's Saying

In the last chapter, I defined process and why it is so crucial for organizational success. In this chapter, I will introduce the concepts of teaching, coaching, and mentoring. I'll explain what they are, how they are different, and why this level of in-depth training can make or break the organization's success. I am sure at times I will sound like a broken record, but I will say it again here: to succeed at training, it is vital to "assume nothing and teach everything."

One of my biggest corporate mentors who helped me understand this concept was George Howard. George was the director of industrial training for the states of South Carolina, Georgia, Florida, and Alabama. He developed each state's industrial training program. In

Alabama, he has a building named for him. As I began to launch my business career, he helped me develop my talent structure, shared some intellectual properties, and introduced me to some friends to get me started with networking. George knew I had a talent, but I needed direction. George gave me that direction. The best part is he mentored me because he sensed I wanted it. I will forever be grateful for his efforts in molding me into the business owner I am today.

FORMAT OF TEACHING

As a leader, it is your responsibility to teach, coach, and mentor your team to achieve the organization's goals. You need to create a strategic plan for those goals to be realized. Consequently, I have created an eight-step format for you to implement so your team will be immersed in a culture of learning. These steps are self-explanatory, but crucial for your team to achieve the desired results:

1. Create a Vision.
2. Establish a Goal.
3. Construct a Plan.
4. Determine a Process.
5. Monitor Results.
6. Hold One-on-Ones with Team Members.
7. Inspect What You Expect.
8. Create a Focus List.

All of these steps have been or will be covered in this book. The bottom line is you must: Teach what you want, how you want it, why you want it, and see that it is done.

When you do this with your mass group of followers, good things will happen. However, keep in mind that because your organization is a production-based business, anyone on your team who deems themselves to be "uncoachable" and does not buy into your company visions needs to perform or you need to convince them it is in their best interest to perform. Your job, first and foremost, is to achieve your goals. Anyone not helping to achieve the goal is a roadblock to the goal and roadblocks are to be eliminated. It is that simple.

COACHING IS LEADERSHIP

A great leader inspires confidence in others and moves them to action. A great coach is a motivator, someone who is able to lay out a plan to help team members achieve goals. When a leader takes time to coach, lines of communication open up, relationships strengthen, goals are attained, and overall team member engagement improves.

Successful leaders at GNP Company "assumed nothing and taught everything" according to their leadership style and philosophy. This philosophy is a process to coordinate getting everyone on the same page relative to goal achievement. I have been coaching leaders at GNP Company for years on this leadership philosophy, and I will share a few highlights with you to help you become even more successful.

Your job as a coach and motivator is to minimize your team members' excuses for failure. Teach and coach your team through the opportunities so they can achieve successful results. Explain the "why" behind the task or project. This explanation will help team members understand more than just the goal itself. Praise team members for small increments of improvement to continue to encourage their performance. Remember to circle back and check-in regularly with your team. Good follow-through on your part is the key to successful coaching. As stated in the leadership philosophy, "Inspect what you expect."

Holding people accountable for job performance or goal attainment is a difficult part of a leader's job. A good leader knows everyone has to perform according to the plan to achieve results. If you believe in the vision, goal, and plan, then you must also believe in your people, their talents, and their ability to achieve results. When you don't believe in your people, things will deteriorate quickly. A great leader knows accountability is a must. Based on what's been taught, don't hold people accountable for something they haven't been taught or if there is no agreed-upon definition of success.

CALL TO ACTION

The next time you are engaged in a conversation with team members regarding task completion, put on your coaching hat and explain the expectation and why it's important; then hold your team members accountable to complete the task by checking in with them regularly. Don't forget to build and strengthen the relationship along the way. Don't be a boss, but incorporate your ideas with theirs. Always look for areas to praise, and make adjustments when needed.

MENTORING THE PROCESS

Getting a good education is an important and necessary part of life. At the same time, receiving on-the-job training can be equally valuable, and in some cases, more valuable.

That said, too many people make the mistake of believing a good education can replace experience or training. Nothing could be further from the truth.

Education and training have radically different results and outcomes. Education provides you with the ability to fully understand something. It teaches you how to empathize. It teaches you *how* to think critically and strategically. Training, however, is about ability and performance. It's about actual mechanics. Formal education and people skills are two different things. You can have all the knowledge, but without people skills, you won't go far when leading a team.

The two aren't meant to oppose or replace one another. In fact, they're meant to work together. When someone is both trained and educated, they become a more valuable worker. They will not only do their job (and do it well), but they also can innovate, solve problems, and progress on their own. Mentor employees who are self-starters with training. Most mentoring is done during the process. Like Mike Tyson says, "Everyone has a plan until they get punched in the mouth." Well, if the process has flaws, it will hit you in the mouth, and that's when the fur starts flying. Then you will learn how to improve your training.

As a leader, you have two responsibilities when it comes to education and training.

First, apply this understanding to your own sense of self-awareness. Don't assume that just because you're educated, you know all there is to know about managing a particular business. Every company has different standards, procedures, and variables that affect how it runs. Let your education guide you, but remain open-minded to gaining valuable, on-the-job experience. Again, there is no guarantee you can do others' jobs better, and you can't see what they see if you haven't walked in their shoes. When you mentor someone, make sure you think together.

Secondly, when it comes to implementing a training program within your company, don't just teach the basic mechanics of a job; educate your employees about the "how" and "why" that comes with that job. Training isn't just about getting an employee to a certain level; it's an ongoing process of development. There is no such thing as one-shot training. Repetition is the mother of all learning. It's important to mentor people on how the human mind plays a role in being successful. Ninety percent of mentoring, coaching, and teaching is from the neck up.

EXERCISE

List one way each that you can teach, coach, and mentor.

_____

_____

_____

SUMMARY

When you implement the format of teaching, coaching, and mentoring as a process, all of your expectations will be clearly communicated and everyone will be on the same page. If team members are not willing to accept what you teach, coach, and mentor, then you lost them somewhere in the vision, goal, and plan stages. People learn differently, so as a leader, you must learn to adjust. When you mentor, you want your employees to make an effort. Ask them, "Why do you think this is the wrong approach? How would you do it? Give me a plan on how you are going to achieve the goal." Beyond coaching, training, and education, mentor by connecting mentally with your employees to create buy-in.

When this happens, it creates beautiful synchronicity and exceptional results, profits, and achieved goals. Then, as the leader, you will be acknowledged for your team's success. Say "Thank you," but give all the praise to your team because they are the closest to the customer and the quality of the product. Without your team, you are nothing; on the other hand, if your team is not doing well, you must take the blame, so don't point fingers. People don't want to hear about the labor pains; they want to see the baby. Get in the coaching and mentorship business and remember that whatever you make or sell, you don't do a product; you do people.

CHAPTER 7

BEING SELF-AWARE AND
MANAGING A DIVERSE WORKFORCE

"Diversity: the art of thinking independently together."

— Malcom Forbes

"People are like apples—apples are different colors,
but they are still apples."

— Isaac's Saying

In the last chapter, I introduced you to teaching, coaching, and mentoring. In this chapter, I will share my belief that these different learning styles can only be effective if you have the ability to communicate your wisdom, experience, knowledge, and company's objectives to a diverse workforce.

THREE REASONS DIVERSITY PLANS FAIL

Diversity in the workplace is more important today than ever before. Many leaders recognize this fact and have put forth initiatives to increase diversity in their businesses.

Despite their good intentions, however, it's not uncommon to see these plans fail. Here are three reasons why:

1. **They're more about checking the boxes:** If your diversity plan reads more like a bullet list of check boxes, then you're approaching it the wrong way. Milestones and broad goals are fine, but your core focus should be more organic and seek to make everyone, managers and employees alike, a part of the effort. Your vision, goal, and plan is a good place to start.

2. **It is all show:** The point of diversity initiatives should be to bring people from different cultures, backgrounds, and lifestyles into your business and make them an integral part of the company—not just another worker or employee. If you're hiring simply to show that you have a "diverse" workforce, but don't actually take your employees' opinions, ideas, and perspectives into consideration, then your plan will ultimately fail. Your one-on-ones are a good place to start to change this situation.

3. **They don't actually celebrate diversity:** Following from the last point, your diversity plan shouldn't seek to make your business into a "melting pot." Diversity initiatives aren't meant to mesh with a "one-size-fits-all" approach. The differences found in a diverse workforce are meant to help your company grow and create more innovative solutions. Each person's unique background and perspective should be celebrated, not assimilated.

WHAT DOES IT MEAN TO BE SELF-AWARE?

Self-awareness isn't a major component of leadership. It's *the* major component. Without self-awareness, you will almost certainly fail as a leader.

For starters, self-awareness is not about knowing what you like or what you want. It's much deeper than that.

Self-awareness is the ability to look within yourself and pinpoint your exact strengths and weaknesses. It's the ability to know where you excel and where you need work. Most importantly, it's the ability to be completely honest and open with yourself about what you realistically can and can't do.

One mistake too many leaders make is letting their passions or wants get in the way of reality—especially when it comes to decision-making. Simply because you "want" something doesn't always mean you should go after it. And if you lack self-awareness, you're more likely to make emotional or knee-jerk decisions that not only impact you, but your employees, your profit, and your entire company.

Speaking of your employees, you should be preaching self-awareness to them as well. In fact, it should be a topic of conversation during every one-on-one. Instilling this value in your employees will help them communicate better with you and other team members, and that will, ultimately, make them more productive.

PRACTICING SELF-AWARENESS

It's important you understand that self-awareness is an ongoing practice. So you need to make a conscious effort to settle down and focus on yourself every day.

A good way to start would be to make a list of your strengths and weaknesses. Remember to be completely honest with yourself. It's not always easy to admit where you need improvement, but it's very important you recognize that you do.

Second, double-check your strengths and make sure you've listed things you're actually good at, not just things you *want* to be good at. It's critical that you realize your passions and strengths might not always line up.

Next, look over your weaknesses. What on that list do you *need* to improve on? Which of your weaknesses affect your day-to-day? Keep in mind that you don't have to master everything. It's perfectly okay to have some weaknesses and surround yourself with other people who excel in those areas so you can learn from them.

Then, go all in on your strengths. Wherever you truly excel, take full advantage of it.

Finally, on your path to self-awareness, it's good to have someone you can communicate with to help you get where you need to be.

NOBODY WANTS TO TALK ABOUT RACE UNTIL IT'S TOO LATE

Like I stated in the quote at the start of this chapter, people are like apples: whether yellow, red, or green, an apple is still an apple. It is the same with people; they are different colors from different origins and backgrounds, but they are still people. So the wisest thing to do as a leader is to clean up your attitude and treat people individually with respect, whether you speak their language or not. People can read your body language. Don't give people a reason not to perform. Doing so is like stepping on your own oxygen cord, and you know what that will do for your career and reputation.

Most companies don't want to talk about race until it is too late. By "too late," I mean it is affecting the brand, consumer, or customer. So let's talk about how to stop the bleeding.

Most people are not comfortable talking about race and diversity for many reasons. For many people, it's like talking about a subject you don't know anything about except for what you learned from TV or from stereotypes. Imagine the room is packed with people waiting for you to deliver a presentation you are prepared for, but then you become so nervous that you couldn't stick a dime in the crack of your tight ass. That's how talking about race makes people feel; as a result, we stay away from this potential powder keg.

Here is what amuses me when companies have a diversity workshop. First, while some companies actually have these workshops on their own, others do it to ward off a new lawsuit, or after one because it has been judge-mandated. Then the person giving the session is "as full of shit as a Thanksgiving turkey." They were born or raised in a predominantly black or white neighborhood, went to a predominantly black or white college, then studied for your presentation and took your money! Did they have a mask on? Because they just robbed you. My point is they don't practice diversity in their own lives, so how can they teach you about it?

In the mentoring process, I talk about diversity right out of the gate. It is easy for me because my friends look like an assorted roll of Life Savers—all completely different colors. If you are racist, it is impossible to hide it; and if you are racist, it is impossible for you to achieve your vision and goal. Your underlying attitudes will eventually show up because you can't hide them forever. So I warn students to clean up their attitudes and treat people individually and not based on their race; you cannot change your perception of people who are different than you overnight, which is why self-awareness is vital.

STEREOTYPES

The workforce is the most integrated place we visit each day, and you have to manage it to be successful and protect your brand. A stereotype is an assumption that all people of a race share the same unattractive qualities. Therefore, the goal is to focus on the goal and not on stereotypes.

According to psychologist and management consultant Dr. Saul W. Gellerman, when you think of people in terms of a stereotype, you are going to find it awfully difficult to get them to credit you with any qualities that do not fit a stereotype about you. It will be hard to get the person to perform for you because you have given them a reason not to perform for you. A leader with a stereotype problem will expose themselves through body image, words, and anything that demeans you in others' eyes, so you can't motivate them. Since the workforce is the most diverse place you visit (in most cases), let's talk about how to bring your team together.

LEADING A DIVERSE WORKFORCE SUCCESSFULLY

Every group has a stereotype about the other because that is the way it is in society. And since society is in your workplace, you have to manage society. Let's use a sports analogy. Take, for example, a football or basketball team. We hear all the time that teams win because of their culture in the locker room and how important that culture is to success or failure. Just like society and your company, the sports locker room is composed of people with different ethnic backgrounds, origins, skin colors, political beliefs, and socio-economic differences. What all these players have in common, regardless of their differences, is the goal: win the game, win the division, win the title! They are on the same page when it comes to the vision, goal, and game plan. You can see them hug each other, kiss each other, cry tears of joy with each other, and tell each other they love each other.

The same thing can happen with your team within your organization. If you can get your team to have the same vision, goal, plan, and process, you will see your results and be able to celebrate like you won the Super Bowl! You see, when a group of people have one common goal, they act as one and not as individuals, so their brains are not occupied by their differences and stereotypes about one another. Your job is to ensure everyone is focused on the goal. After work, most people segregate, but you have to make sure they work on the goal when they are at work.

Your one-on-ones with your team members will give you the opportunity to talk about the game plan, goal, and their part in the team's success. Your one-on-one gives you the opportunity to build a relationship with your team to send the message that they are important, which builds your credibility and respect. You will then influence how each person is motivated and you can use that motivation to help build the team's success. You will find you have more in common with people from diverse backgrounds than you think, and those commonalities will make you and your team members want to support each other. Granted, some leaders are who they are; they won't change, and their employees will usually leave their companies fast. Now that you know better, you can prevent that from happening to your team.

UNDERSTANDING MILLENNIALS

Today, Baby Boomers are retiring; they will be entirely out of the workforce by 2035. Meanwhile, Millennials are the biggest and fastest-growing segment of the labor market. Millennials constitute anyone born between 1980 and 2000. Millennials are the most diverse group ever to come through America. If you don't believe me, look at the companies that advertise for them to buy their products.

Lydia Abbott wrote an amazing article about Millennials that I thought was perfect for people learning to manage a diverse workforce. Not only are you trying to manage sex, race, and religion, but today, you are also trying to manage a younger workforce that most likely thinks and acts differently from you. Abbott's article is titled: "8 Millennial Traits You Should Know About Before Your Hire Them."[1] I encourage you to read the entire article, but here are the traits in a nutshell.

1.   Multi-taskers: They can juggle many responsibilities at once.

2.   Connected: They know everything about social media because it is their life.

3.   Tech-Savvy: They are the most technologically advanced generation.

4.   Want Instant Gratification and Recognition: They grew up with constant praise and need it.

5.   Desire Flexibility and Work/Life Balance: They work hard but also want to play hard.

6.   Team-Oriented: They love building friendships.

7.   Open and Honest with Management: They want their opinion heard and valued.

8.   Career Advancement: They want to move up and be promoted.

---

1. Available at: https://business.linkedin.com/talent-solutions/blog/2013/12/8-millennials-traits-you-should-know-about-before-you-hire-them. Accessed July 1, 2021.

In my experience managing and leading this generation, Lydia has nailed these characteristics. I encourage you not to be intimidated by Millennials' many skills and talents. Rather, I challenge you to leverage their skills and talents for the betterment of your organization en route to achieving the goals and vision your company seeks.

Be like Henry Ford. As I mentioned before, when Henry Ford built Ford Motor Company from the ground up, he consistently hired people who were more talented and more educated than him. Then he turned them loose to execute his goals and vision to build the number-one auto manufacturer in the world during his industry's infancy. Hence, I challenge you to embrace Millennials' skills and characteristics and not be intimated by their wisdom and abilities. Have them put their skills to use to build your organization; then you will succeed together as a team.

MILLENNIALS ARE TRIANGLES

One of my colleagues, Cary Tutelman, is the author of *The Balance Point*. Cary wrote a terrific article on Millennials and gave me permission to share it with you in its entirety here. (For more information on Cary, visit TutelmanConsulting.com.)

If Millennials are Triangles, Here's How to Smooth Angles

When we talk about millennials in the workforce, we mention how they are tech savvy people who have trouble with rigid timelines and schedules, need instant gratifications and recognition, are impatient with the status quo and are self-absorbed. But I think of millennials as triangles.

I call them triangles because they have pointy, sharp, rigid sides. When they come into the workforce, their pointy, sharp sides tear at the fabric of workforce etiquette and time-honored standards of communication and behavior. This causes conflict and frustrations with others, especially their older peers and supervisors.

But I don't blame these triangles. Their behavior and communication comes from their sense of what is normal. Furthermore, I think every generation produces a group of young adults whose values and ways are different than those of the "establishment."

I, myself, am a baby boomer. When we were young adults, we thought that all you needed was love, while the establishment thought that what we needed was hard work and respect for our elders. We were triangles too.

Since our youth, most of us have grown and matured. We have become hexagons. Our pointy, sharp edges have been smoothed by experience, maturity and adapting to workplace etiquette and standards. As hexagons, most of us move pretty smoothly through the fabric of the American workforce.

A great man once said that the youth, "have bad manners, contempt for authority; they show disrespect for elders and love chatter in place of exercise." That man was Socrates and his quote is around 2400 years old. This idea of youth as bucking the establishment goes back a long way. It must be the natural order of things.

It seems to me, then, that each generation produces a group of youth who started their adulthood as triangles. In the workforce, most of us transition from triangles to hexagons, forming and refining our identities and values and also adapting at work. It's called the maturing process.

So what is noteworthy about Millennials is not that they have different ways. It is how they react to us and how we work with them.

Employers need to understand that the Millennials do bring a valuable perspective to the workplace. Being tech savvy and focusing on social media are good examples. It is, for us non-Millennials, a new way of communicating, reaching out to people and staying connected. We must embrace and explore these new ideas.

The Millennials need to understand they have a lot to learn from those of us who have transitioned from triangles to hexagons. This is because we proved that we could have strong identities and values and still be successful at work. Smoothing our rough edges was a key to our long-term success in the workplace and it is the key for Millennials, too. It wasn't easy, but we realized it was necessary.

Some people do remain triangles and are very successful. We call them entrepreneurs, artists, mavericks, etc. But the rest of us join the workforce and have to find a way to maintain our identity and adapt to our surroundings. We all have to decide how much rounding we can accept and where we draw the line. For some of us, this is a lifetime process. Others of us figure it out quickly.

So how do we help Millennials in the workplace? Initially, let's not be too hard on them. They are us. Sometimes we forget this. Millennials need mentors who have been through the transition process and can help them make good choices. They don't flourish in an environment where people just criticize their youthful ways and differences. And remember, they have good ideas just like we did.

But Millennials should not get a pass either. Just because they are the future, we shouldn't give them a wide berth for their pointy, sharp edges. Nor should we coddle them and turn ourselves inside out to accommodate them. We can help the best by:

1. Giving them immediate feedback on the effect they are having on others.

2. Teaching them to understand and respect others' perspectives.

3. Teaching them how to effectively present ideas to others.

4. Teaching them how to convert their impatience into productive action.

In the end, they need to do the development work we did, struggle the way we did and earn the success we got. This is what business owners want and it is the natural order of things.

I encourage you to digest this article. Read it a few times and do what you can to take the lessons offered in it to your organization. Your role as a leader is to positively influence people to follow you (Millennials included), and the best way that can happen is to have them view you as a kind, fair, unbiased leader who cares equally about all people. When you treat everyone the same, drama is removed from your workforce, and then everyone can focus on achieving results for the team.

EXERCISE

Write out a diversity statement below stating how you will honor all your employees regardless of sex, race, religion, etc.

_____

_____

_____

SUMMARY

To succeed in leadership, you need to be self-aware. Part of being self-aware is being aware of whether or not you have diversity in your workplace and whether you are promoting it. The best way to be self-aware is to recognize both your strengths and weaknesses and then work on those things you need to improve.

The best way to manage diversity is to eliminate all stereotypes and treat everyone the same. When you do this, your team will like you; remember, people follow those they like and respect. It is that simple.

Additionally, your role is to break down barriers within your workforce in regards to racism. You need to find a way to leave this issue outside of your organization's workforce and create a safe place for your workers not just to survive, but to thrive in your environment. Insist that your subordinates become a team; forget the socio-economic issues that the media focuses on, and get all your team to focus on the organization's goals!

CHAPTER 8

KNOWING YOUR ROLE AND NURTURING RELATIONSHIPS

"Do what you did in the beginning of a relationship
and there won't be an end."

— Anthony Robbins

"All results depend upon relationships."

— Isaac's Saying

In the last chapter, I shared my experiences with how to manage a diverse workforce to achieve organizational goals. I am sure you have heard what Robert Kiyosaki said about relationships and networking: "Your network determines the size of your net worth." This is especially true in the corporate world and the manufacturing customer service arena. If you are unable to completely understand your role, develop your own skills, and listen to the needs of all your employees, you will either have these employees undermine you, leading to poor worker satisfaction, or you will be one of the reasons for high turnover. If either situation exists, you will struggle to achieve your goals as a leader.

YOUR LEADERSHIP ROLE AND REQUIREMENTS

Being the leader and supervising can be an exhilarating and rewarding experience. It provides means for growth and opportunities. You can fulfill powerful psychological needs by supervising. But you really have to want it, more than any other job you can fill. You have to possess a healthy desire to exercise power in constructive ways. You have to want to influence others, and you have to be prepared to gain personal satisfaction vicariously through others' achievements.

If you accept a supervisory position just for the money or prestige, you may be headed for trouble. Your primary reason should be your desire to lead and serve, to be in charge, and to achieve a higher level of authority and responsibility.

If you are still attached to your old job, you may think you can keep your hands in it. If you think you can cover your supervisory responsibilities by coming to work earlier and staying later, think again. Supervising does not mean working harder or longer; it means working differently and working smarter.

THE TRANSITION FROM DOING TO SUPERVISING

When you are promoted to a supervisor or leadership role for the first time, you leave one world and enter another. You must make a major shift in roles. When you were not a leader, you were only responsible for your own performance and no one else's. You were an expert at what you did. You took pride in personal achievement. You made virtues of perfection, meticulous preparation, and complete self-reliance. And you did it all yourself. However, if you cling to these old ways when you supervise, you could end up getting fired. You must shed those self-centered habits and take on some new ones that are focused on your team.

Your mindset must shift from your own personal achievement to that of your subordinates. You can no longer afford to be the "do-it-yourselfer." Yes, there will be times when you must pitch in to help your subordinates' work, but those times should be exceptions. If you routinely pitch in, you will neglect your own work.

Because you are now a part of management, you must be more responsive to your boss, your fellow supervisors, and other players. You must now integrate your activities and touch base with more people than you did in the past. You will have to cultivate a close relationship with your boss and build rapport with other key people in your organization. You will spend a good portion of your time coping with these demands. That's all the more reason you can't afford to be doing the wrong kind of work.

PERFORMING YOUR ROLE WHILE BUILDING RELATIONSHIPS

You have many roles as a supervisor. Your position defines your formal supervisory role. Implicit to that are many sub-roles that, at any one time, may emerge to become the predominant one. Included are the sub-roles of the authority figure, leader, enforcer, counselor, coach, etc. Other separate roles emerge as the situation demands. At times, your role will be that of follower (when dealing with your boss or serving as a member of a team), peer, or client. You will also take on some informal roles such as grapevine communicator, mentor, protégé, and confidante. This constant shifting of roles requires you to quickly adapt to the role required by the situation—especially when responding to your leader. Proper role-playing requires skills in perception, empathy, and an ability to relate to people—basically, human skills.

YOUR REQUIRED SKILLS

Regardless of your position in your organization's hierarchy, you and your other managers all must bring three major skills to your job: technical skills, human skills, and conceptual skills.

The degree of each skill required varies with levels of management. Often, managers are only focused on technical or human skills and lack conceptual skills. Given that you were hired or offered the promotion, you are assumed to be pretty competent in the technical aspects of your job. But you (like so many of us) probably could use more skill in the human relations arena. The bottom line is you will increasingly depend on others for results. You are going to become more involved in leading, communicating, and motivating. So, keep in mind that one major reason supervisors are fired is an inability to relate to people. Let's talk about how to boost your skills in relating well to others. And by the way, you can apply these skills to all areas of your life, not just your work.

BUILDING EFFECTIVE HUMAN RELATIONSHIPS

Building relationship skills is so extremely vital for you and all front-line supervisors. You will spend most of your time in face-to-face contact with people. A list of desirable attributes needed for effective human relations would be endless, but here are five personal qualities a supervisor should develop:

1. **Empathy:** Empathy is the ability to see others' points of view without necessarily agreeing with them.

2. **Self-Awareness:** Self-awareness is having a good sense of your values, your confidence, your leadership style, and your personal inhibitions.

3. **Acceptance of Individual Differences:** This type of acceptance is the realization that everyone should not be respected alike, but within the context of their values and personalities.

4. **Perceptual Awareness:** Perceptual awareness is the understanding that you and others view the world differently.

5. **Focusing on People:** This type of focus is your commitment to holding high expectations for people's achievement and treating them as responsible adults.

COMMUNICATING EXPECTATIONS

The challenge with placing expectations on others is they often don't meet those expectations, and then you become disappointed. For that reason, I never try to place expectations on people outside of work, but at work, expectations need to be accurately communicated so everyone can be on the same page working toward one shared goal. The bottom line regarding expectations is that a large part of your job involves focusing on people. The expectations we hold for people (not only for subordinates), but everyone we interact with, are rooted in how we treat them.

The following quote clearly drives this point home. It is spoken by Eliza Doolittle in George Bernard Shaw's play *Pygmalion*.

> …the difference between a lady and a flower girl is not how she behaves, but how she is treated. I shall always be a flower girl to Professor Higgins, because he always treats me as a flower girl, and always will; but I know I can be a lady to you, because you always treat me as a lady, and always will.

BECOMING A GREAT SUPERVISOR

You can become a great manager or supervisor by doing the following four things well:

1. **Studying Your Organization:** This requires knowing your organization's mission, value, and goals, accurately communicating them, and encouraging your team to buy into these metrics and work toward the common goals.

2. **Using Past Experience on the Job:** This requires applying all the wisdom from your past experience on the job (both good and bad) to effectively lead your team.

3. **Emulating What Good Managers Do:** This includes looking at and studying both the positives and negatives of what other managers do and seeing how their teams react to these behaviors.

4. **Conducing One-on-Ones Effectively:** These are meetings in your office behind closed doors with your subordinates, one at a time. In these meetings, you do all you can to learn from them their personal goals, challenges, strengths, and weaknesses. Also, you learn about their family situations (like hobbies, kids' names, what they like, birthdays, etc.) so you can best support them in those areas as well. In these meetings, you can come up with strategies to mentor, teach, and support them on their paths to success.

This reminds me of Theodore Roosevelt's quote:

> "People don't care how much you know
> until they know how much you care."

That's an important concept to remember, so I'll remind you of it a few more times before you finish this book.

EXERCISE

List three ways you will strengthen and nourish your relationships with both your bosses and your subordinates.

_____

_____

_____

SUMMARY

As a first-level supervisor, you are the closest management contact with the workforce. Therefore, you must have the technical skill at the level of the work being done. This is very important because your workers cannot be too much farther advanced in technology than you, or they may lose respect for you. Unless you know the right questions to ask, they can be smarter.

But above all, you must possess interpersonal skills since you are now expected to get results that support the organization's goals. You must also be skilled in getting the work done. This is the process, the art, of managing and being an effective leader. The better you are at encompassing these attributes, the better you can support your organization's overall vision and goals.

MOTIVATION

"If you set goals and go after them with all the determination you can muster, your gifts will take you places that will amaze you."

— Les Brown

"Motivation is the desire to achieve something so bad that it become so habit forming that you expand your mental capabilities and confidence to levels you never thought you had and you keep achieving."

— Isaac's Saying

CHAPTER 9

LISTENING AND COMMUNICATING THE VISION

"One of the most sincere forms of respect is actually listening to what another has to say."

— Bryant H. McGill

"When you listen to employees, you get to know the person and the employee, which is vital to the success of you both."

— Isaac's Saying

In the last chapter, I discussed the importance of your ability to nurture your employee relationships. In this chapter, I will explain how to be successful at listening to the needs of your subordinates as their supervisor, and then communicating the vision of your organization to them so they can help you achieve the goals at hand. Without solid communication in your work environment, it is almost impossible to achieve the large profits you and your management team have put in place. When you properly communicate, you are actually motivating your team members to work harder and become even more a part of the team.

ROLE OF COMMUNICATIONS

Communication is one of the most important topics since a failure to communicate effectively is regarded as one of management's key problems. Extra attention should be given to the significance of effective communication because it will make your job as leader easier.

As a leader, you know that using communication is constant in your job. In fact, you probably spend as much as 85 percent of your time as a communicator. Every day, you are engaged in a variety of communication activities: memos, emails, and reports; talking on the phone; conducting meetings; directing employees; and training employees. All of this is done to communicate goals, objectives, and plans so employees will know where they are headed and what their functions are relative to what others are doing. You should be giving people the necessary information for them to do their jobs properly and to encourage and promote interest in their jobs.

Effective communication also relates to your personnel management responsibilities as a leader. For example: Performance standards must be understood by employees; they must know what is expected of them. During the annual appraisal and counseling session, both the employee and the leader must be able to communicate their goals and expectations. Remember, in Chapter 7 we talked about the goal to work as a team.

Questions to an employee must be stated clearly so the leader can listen and respond to the answers given. Leaders must be sure the employee understands what kind of information is needed and why. On-the-job training requires good instructions from the leader. The leader must listen to the employee's self-development goals and be able to counsel the employee.

Grievances and complaints require skills in listening actively to determine whether employees are communicating any hidden messages. Example: You may be listening to or noticing body language from an employee when discussing a situation. You might then ask the employee, "When your leaders asked you to change this, how did it make you feel?" Sometimes, you can detect hidden messages in the answer that will lead you to other places.

The leader's attitude plays an important role here and communicates interest or lack of it. Recognition of employee accomplishments and a sincere interest in employee welfare communicates awareness and encourages motivation and self-confidence in employees along with building relationships.

Studies have shown that improving communication can contribute to higher morale, lower absenteeism, lower turnover, and higher productivity.

Without effective communication, it is almost impossible to drive people toward the organization's purpose. Therefore, the goal is always to focus on improving your communication skills. Doing so will make your job as a leader much easier.

WHAT IS COMMUNICATION?

Communication can be defined as a behavior that transmits meaning from one person (the sender) to another (the receiver). Words, facial expressions, and gestures are forms of communication because they transmit feelings, facts, and ideas to someone else. Communication is the only transmission that results in an exchange of meaning and information. The definition does not specify what is good or bad communication.

Now, we must answer: What is effective person-to-person communication? Simply stated, interpersonal communication occurs when the sender is reasonably certain the receiver accurately understands the message. Real communication moves freely in both directions from the sender to the receiver and from the receiver to the sender.

Even though we have been communicating since birth, we usually do not stop to consider how the communication process works. To increase our understanding of this process, let's look at the one-on-one communication process.

MODEL OF THE COMMUNICATION PROCESS

1. The sender communicates from their own purpose, feelings, needs, values, and frame of reference.

2. The sender has certain objectives that help achieve the basic purpose.

3. The sender must establish what they will say and how much.

4. The sender transmits the message both verbally and non-verbally (words, gestures, facial or body expressions, emotions).

5. The receiver translates or decodes the message by interpreting it in terms of past experiences.

6. The receiver sends a message back in terms of their behavior, both verbally and non-verbally.

7. The receiver sends feedback information that helps the sender know whether the message is received properly. The sender often must request feedback to check understanding.

8. People interpret messages differently when the message has some meaning to both sender and receiver.

9. Effective communication occurs when the message has the same meaning to both the sender and receiver.

THE MEANING OF ACTIVE LISTENING

One basic responsibility of the leader or executive is the development, adjustment, and integration of individual employees. Leaders try to develop employee potential, delegate responsibility, and achieve cooperation. To do so, they must have the ability to listen intelligently and actively to those they work with. When they are successful, amazing things can be achieved.

Active listening is an important way to bring about change in people. Despite the popular notion that listening is a passive approach, clinical and research evidence clearly shows that sensitive listening is the most effective agent for individual personality change and group development. Listening brings about changes in people's attitudes toward themselves and others, and it also brings about changes in their basic values and personal philosophy. People who have been listened to in this new and special way become more emotionally mature, more open to their experiences, less defensive, more democratic, and less authoritarian.

When people are listened to sensitively, they tend to listen with more care and make clear exactly what they are feeling and thinking. Group members tend to listen more to each other, become less argumentative, and become more ready to incorporate others' viewpoints. Because listening reduces the threat of having one's ideas criticized, the person being listened to is better able to see the other person and the situation each for what it is, and therefore, is more likely to feel their contributions are worthwhile.

Not the least important result of listening is the change that takes place within the listener. Besides the fact that listening provides more information than any other activity, it also builds deep positive relationships and tends to constructively alter the listener's attitudes. Listening is a growth experience.

HOW TO LISTEN

Active listening aims to bring about changes in people. To achieve this end, it relies upon definite techniques—things to do and things to avoid doing. Before discussing these techniques, we should understand how the individual personality develops. All humans grow and evolve differently, based on numerous factors and the environment in which they are raised. Remember all of society is represented in your workforce.

From early childhood, we learn to think of ourselves in certain, very definite ways. We have all built up pictures in our lives. Sometimes, these self-pictures are pretty realistic, but other times, they are not. For example, a middle-aged overweight woman may fancy herself as a youthful, ravishing siren, or an awkward teenage boy may regard himself as an athlete.

All of us have experiences that fit the way we think about ourselves. But it is much harder to accept experiences that don't fit. And sometimes, if it is very important for us to hang on to this self-portrait, we don't accept or admit these experiences at all.

These self-portraits are not necessarily attractive. A man, for example, may view himself as incompetent and worthless. He may feel he is doing his job poorly despite favorable job reviews by his employer. As long as he has these feelings, he must deny any experiences that would not seem to fit his self-portrait; in this case, that might indicate to him that he is competent. It is so necessary for him to maintain this self-portrait that he is threatened by anything that would tend to change it. Thus, when the company raises his salary, it may seem to him to be only additional proof that he is a fraud. He must also hold onto this self-portrait, because good or bad, it is the only thing he has by which to identify himself.

FIVE LISTENING TECHNIQUES FOR BETTER RESULTS

1. **Know What to Avoid:** When we encounter a person with a problem, our usual response is to try to change their way of looking at things—to get them to see the situation the way we see it, or how we would like them to see it. We plead, reason, scold, encourage, insult, or prod—anything to bring about change in their desired direction, which is in the direction we want them to travel. What we seldom realize, however, is that under these circumstances, we are usually responding to our own needs to see the world in certain ways. It is always difficult to tolerate and understand actions that are different from the ways we believe people should act. If, however, we can free ourselves from the need to influence and direct others, we can enable ourselves to listen with understanding and, thereby, employ the most potent available agent of change.

2. **From Their Point of View:** Active listening requires that you get inside the speaker, that you grasp just what they are communicating from their viewpoint. More than that, you must convey to the speaker that you are seeing things from their viewpoint. To listen actively means that you must employ this understanding. Then tie it to the vision, goal, plan, and results and talk about adjustments in your one-on-one meetings.

3. **Listen for Total Meaning:** Any message a person tries to get across has two components: the content of the message and the feeling or attitude underlying the content. Both are important, and both give the message meaning. This total meaning of the message is what you try to understand. For example, Lamar comes to his foreman and says, "I've finished that machine setup." This message has obvious content and perhaps calls upon the foreman for another work assignment. Suppose, on the other hand, he says "Well, I am finally finished with that dang machine setup." The message's content is the same, but the message has changed—and changed in an important way both for foreman and worker. Here, sensitive listening can facilitate the relationship. Suppose the foreman were to respond simply by giving another assignment. Would the employee feel he got his total message across? Would he feel free to talk to his foreman? Would he feel better about his job, or just be more anxious about doing good work on the next assignment? Now, on the other hand, if the foreman were to respond with "Glad to have it over with, huh?" or "Had a pretty rough time of it?" or "Guess you won't like doing

anything like that again?", then he is telling the worker he heard him and understands. It doesn't necessarily mean the next work assignment needs to be changed or that he must spend an hour listening to the worker complain about the setup problems he encountered. He may do a number of things differently in light of the new information he has from the worker—but not necessarily. Just a little extra sensitivity on the part of the foreman can transform an average working climate into a good one. Responding and following up help build relationships and send the message that you care and the employee is important.

4. **Respond to Feelings:** In some instances, the content is far less important than the feeling underlying it. To catch the full flavor of the message's meaning, you must respond particularly to the feeling component. If, for instance, Lamar had said, "I'd like to melt this machine down and make paperclips out of it," responding to content would be obviously absurd. But responding to his disgust or anger in trying to work with his machine recognizes the meaning of his message. Each time, the listener must try to remain sensitive to the total meaning the message has for the speaker. Ask yourself, "What is he trying to tell me? What does this mean to him? How does he see this situation?" To walk in the speaker's shoes for a while, you will need to be in this mindset while doing your one-on-ones, which we'll talk about later in Chapter 21.

5. **Note All Cues:** Not all communication is verbal. The speaker's words alone do not tell us everything they are communicating. And hence, truly sensitive listening re-

quires that we become aware of several kinds of communication besides verbal. The way a speaker hesitates in their speech can tell us much more about their feelings. So, too, can the inflection of their voice. They may stress certain parts loudly and clearly, while they may mumble others. We should also note such things as the person's facial expressions, body posture, hand movements, eye movements, and breathing. All of these help convey the total message.

WHAT WE COMMUNICATE BY LISTENING

The first reaction most people have when they consider listening as a possible method for dealing with other people is that listening can't be sufficient in itself. Because listening is passive, they feel that listening does not communicate anything to the speaker. Actually, nothing could be further from the truth.

By constantly listening to a speaker, you are conveying to them "I'm interested in you as a person and I think what you feel is important. I respect your thoughts, and even if I don't agree with them, I know they are valid for you. I feel sure you have a contribution to make. I am not trying to change you or evaluate you. I just want to understand you. I think you are worth listening to, and I want you to know I am the kind of person you can talk to."

The subtle but more important aspect of listening is it demonstrates that the message works. While it is difficult to convince someone you respect them by telling them so, you are much more likely to get this message across by really behaving that way—by actually having and demonstrating respect for the person. Listening does this more effectively. Keep this fact in mind when changing your culture and leadership style.

Like other behavior, listening is contagious. This contagion has implications for all communication problems, whether between two people, or within a large organization. To ensure good communication between associates up and down the line, you must take responsibility for setting a pattern of listening. Just as anger is usually met with anger, argument with argument, and deception with deception, listening can be met with listening. Every person who feels responsibility in a situation can set the tone of the interaction. The important lesson here is that any behavior exhibited by one person will eventually be responded to with similar behavior in the other person. Remember this point because it could be the key to eliminating all fighting, yelling, door slamming, screaming, etc. This a vital concept to understand and implement. Remember, you get what you put out there.

Listening is a constructive behavior, but if one's attitude is to "wait out" the speaker rather than really listen, it will fail. The person who consistently listens with understanding is the one who, eventually, is most likely to be listened to. My point is if you really want to be heard and understood by another, you can develop that person as a potential listener, ready for new ideas, provided you can first develop yourself in these ways and sincerely listen with understanding and respect.

EXERCISE

List two ways you can become a better listener. Then list two ways you can improve your communication skills.

_____

_____

_____

_____

_____

_____

_____

_____

SUMMARY

When you, as the leader, manager, or supervisor of your team, actively listen to your subordinates' needs and clearly communicate your organization's goals, amazing things will happen. Your team becomes motivated, and a motivated workforce performs better and, hence, achieves company objectives. As I have always said, turnover and absenteeism are symptoms of not listening or motivating. Stop chasing symptoms because not listening and not motivating are root causes.

People are more effectively motivated when given some freedom in how they do their work compared to when every action is prescribed in advance. They do better when some degree of decision-making about their jobs is possible than when all the decisions are made for them. As leaders, you need to listen to these needs and properly communicate both organizational goals and areas where they are free to creatively achieve the desired results. Your team will respond more adequately when they are treated as personalities rather than as cogs in a machine. In short, if the ego motivations of self-determination, self-expression, or a sense of personal worth can be tapped, the individual will be more effectively motivated and energized. And that is it in a nutshell, people. How you improve profits is through people. It feels good when that happens for the people I mentor.

The use of external sanctions, or pressure for production, may work to some degree, but not to the extent that the more internalized motives do. When individuals come to identify themselves with their jobs and the work of their groups, human resources are much more fully used in the production process. As a result of this active listening and proper communication, company goals are realized and corporate profits are earned.

CHAPTER 10

SETTING GOALS AND
EXECUTING THE PLAN

"Unless commitment is made, there are only
promises and hopes; but no plans."

— Peter Drucker

"Hope is like an anchor; it's fixed on the unseen."

— Isaac's Saying

In the last chapter, we talked about communicating and listening.
In this chapter, we will discuss how to execute the plan you have
created or are in the midst of creating. Also in this chapter, I will
give you an extensive case study of how some of my clients used the
five steps to increase their productivity and profits. Peter Drucker's
above quote is very pertinent to this chapter, but another thought
leader who drives this point home well is Harvey Mackay, author
of *Swim With the Sharks Without Being Eaten Alive*. Mackay said:
"Ideas without actions are worthless." I wholeheartedly agree.

GETTING THE WHOLE TEAM INVOLVED

The best way to get your whole team involved is to share the vision
so all your subordinates will be on the same page. As the leader, it

is your responsibility to communicate the vision of the corporation so all your team members' daily actions can be aligned with management's goals. This is a process of communicating, planning, executing, following process, grinding, developing positive work habits, and then creating a seamless repetition where all are working in harmony toward the same outcomes.

Next, it is your responsibility to set the pace. In essence, you are the rabbit, and people will follow at the speed the rabbit moves forward. But know this: Once the rabbit quits, all those who follow quit as well. So if you get the whole team to buy in, as the pacesetter, you can't quit. Finish what you start. Be like a postage stamp: Stick to something until you get there.

HAVING CONSISTENCY IN PLACE

As the leader, you must create a culture of consistency where you and your team do the right thing every day. In a sense, you are creating an example for your workers to follow to execute goals and policies. Repetition is the mother of all learning. However, if your consistency goal is to work, you need to treat everyone on your team the same, regardless of race, sex, religion, or upbringing. The same is true when it comes to respect. But you can't treat them the same when it comes to the work itself; instead, treat them according to whether they are doing good or bad work. It is okay for you to have different values than some of your workers outside of work, but at work, you must put all that aside (remember, society is represented in your workforce), and treat all with the same consistency. Then you will consistently be able to lead your team to set the right goals and execute the plan management would like your team and you to follow. We covered this point previously in Chapter 7 when we discussed diversity in the workplace.

HAVING MENTAL AND PHYSICAL CAPABILITIES

If someone can do a job after it is well-defined and achieve the goal set through proper training, then that person has the physical or mental capability to do that job. Bottom line: Not all of your employees are graced with the same level of intelligence or physical strength. Let's face it; everyone is different. As a result, some people can't perform the job they are assigned. When this is the case, it is your responsibility to develop them or match them internally with a better position that suits their strengths. Safety on the job must always be your number-one goal, so if you have workers who put others at risk, you must act swiftly and remove them to preserve your safe working environment for all your workers. If your employees come to work with ten fingers and toes, it is your responsibility to make sure they go home each night with ten fingers and toes.

MEASURING YOUR PROGRESS

There's an old saying that is so applicable to this section's title: "You can't improve that which you don't measure!" Truth has never been so clear. For this reason, in Chapter 17, I will introduce you to Key Performance Indicators (KPIs) as a tool to help you measure your progress. There should be daily reports in both red and green posted to show daily progress toward the goal you set for your team. Red means progress isn't happening and green means success. Measuring also helps with communication and educating others on the process.

MAPPING AND UNDERSTANDING COMMON PURPOSE

In Chapter 5, I talked about the importance of knowing the process and sticking to it. The strategy of mapping and understanding the common purpose becomes visible when you and your team execute the plan by applying the process to achieve your goals and vision.

When your team understands the organization's common goal and purpose, provided they are capable, they will do a good job based on what is being taught to help you achieve the desired goal. However, if they are capable and understand the common purpose, but they still don't perform, you must act accordingly. Review who was the teacher and how the strategy was taught to ensure the task is as simple as possible, according to the student, not the teacher. As a leader, you are looking for effort.

I use the phrase "error repeater" to describe a subordinate who gets two leaders fired before the subordinate actually learns their job. To prevent this situation, it is so very important to get all team members to understand the common purpose. When you get buy-in, certainly less people will be terminated, and hence, more people will be available to execute the desired goals. Your job is to develop talent, not get rid of people you didn't teach or someone you taught only once or twice, the exception being if it is a safety issue. We cannot tolerate safety violations in any job.

KNOWING WHAT TO CHANGE

As a leadership coach, I am a big fan of a three-step process one of my coaching peers, Patrick Snow, teaches his clients: Trial and Error, Test and Measure, and Rinse and Repeat.

Teaching change could be done seven different ways by seven different people. For this reason, I always say: Assume nothing; teach everything. If you don't have the physical and mental capabilities to do your job, you can't stay here. Most leaders fail in their jobs because they go in without a plan. Putting out fires and complaining does not work. So, in order to know what to change, it is important that you, as the leader, know exactly what your goals are in your department.

Everyone on your team needs to have a goal because you cannot be successful without one, and change will never occur successfully without goals. You need buy-in from your team and you need everyone to work toward achieving the same KPIs. Every leader needs to have a goal based on the scorecard. When everyone focuses on a common goal, they celebrate wins as a team and they get together as a team to discuss failures and correct them.

One challenge with change is that employee turnover is so fast that we throw people into the fire, but don't teach. Keep everyone's eyes on the goal. Do not treat people who do good work the same as the people who do bad work. You need to treat both with respect, but you also need to let people know when they are doing good or bad work and reward or discipline them accordingly.

Also, to manage change, you need to create and communicate deadlines to spur action for things to keep moving. If you miss a deadline, you must ask, "Why?" What's more important than something your leader asks you to do? You must have discipline to be good at what you do; remember, people will mimic you. And that helps the culture.

UNDERSTANDING THE GOALS

As the team leader, you will need to bind your team together with the vision of your departmental goals and organizational goals. If business were a sport, the way to win your game would be to turn a profit, have a healthy and safe work environment, and deliver high quality products and services to the customer. And to achieve the metrics, it is your responsibility to get everyone to buy into the vision! This is one leadership style, and one philosophy, that must be bought into by your subordinates if the organization's goals are to be achieved.

HOW TO SET A GOAL
(AND WHAT ARE YOU WILLING TO ACCOMPLISH?)

Connecting to your vision for success, and determining what you are willing to accomplish is first and foremost. The things you are willing to accomplish must be very well defined and set forth with a passion to achieve them. You cannot measure what you cannot see! Most people are not well-trained in achieving goals at home or at work, and the formal education system doesn't teach dreams and passion. That's where mentors and parents come in.

Congratulations! You now are the mentor and coach of goal setting. The best way to mentor your team on goal setting is to lead by example from your successes in achieving personal and business goals. Those goals will give your team an indication of what to expect, how to act when overcoming adversity, and how to reward themselves with small victories on the way to the ultimate prize. It will give them a new perspective on how to manage time, delegate, plan, inspect their work, and many other important things that goal setting can bring into a person's life to help make them successful.

Make sure you cover in full detail what procrastination can do to goals and dreams, and the importance of staying focused and positive every day. Goal setters usually know how to motivate themselves, but teaching your team how to set goals and achieve them will help you and your team be more successful in the long run. Happy teaching! It's a lost art in most companies.

EXERCISE

List three major goals you have in your personal or business life. Next, add three action plans you will implement to achieve these goals.

_____

_____

_____

_____

_____

_____

SUMMARY

The best way to set your goals and execute your plans is to get your team involved, be consistent, evaluate your team's individual skill sets, apply a common purpose, and finally, measure your progress. When you find people or processes that deviate from your ability to lead and achieve results, you must be willing to implement changes so you can ultimately achieve your organization's goals.

If you are struggling with this process, I strongly encourage you to inspect the details of your plan and how it is being executed or communicated by its teacher. Next, minimize excuses and finish the task at hand.

Setting goals and executing them can be summed up by this statement: The true measure of success is once you put the fire out, don't let it recur!

CHAPTER 11

INVOLVING
DIRECT REPORTS

"Ask less often: 'What's in it for me?' and ask often:
'What's in me for it?'"

— John Ed Mathison

"Influence people to be a part of something bigger than
themselves. If not, people won't achieve their goals.
Succeeding at influencing others is an art."

— Isaac's Saying

In the last chapter, I talked about the importance of executing your plan. However, we usually can't execute it alone. For the best results, we need to elicit others' support. Get others to buy into your vision. Involve not only your direct reports, but your entire team in the execution of your plan. We will discuss how to get that involvement in this chapter and the next one.

GETTING DIRECT REPORTS ON THE SAME PAGE

If you are unwilling to confront, you are unwilling to lead. But, confront nicely. True leaders mean what they say, and say what they mean. Their conversations are planned and followed by committed action. I call these difficult conversations because they create mutual understanding. Good leaders are not afraid to talk about the tough things. They have difficult conversations because they know that burying problems doesn't make them go away.

YOU CAN'T RUN THE RACE ALONE

As a leader, achieving your goals is extremely vital to your career success and the satisfaction of winning. Good leaders know they cannot run the race alone; it takes a team effort to be successful in achieving desired results. For this to happen, the leader must have a vision of what success looks like and incorporate goals to achieve that vision. (By success, I mean what drives the business from a revenue standpoint, not a mission statement.)

To avoid micromanaging your direct reports, you must understand how to effectively communicate, motivate, and educate direct reports on the vision and goals (see Chapter 9 on communication). The first step is to ask your direct reports what their vision and goals for success are in their particular departments or region. Next, you need to have a high-level discussion about the vision and goal to make sure you see the same target for success that drives their department or region. If your visions don't match, or only partly match, it opens up a chance to educate each other on the business; then, with a shared vision, you both become successful because you are attached at the hip when it comes to accountability. No boss is in the room when you have this session because you are looking for buy-in, so put your boss hat (and negative attitude if you have one) away! This session begins the process of including people to help you become successful by involving them in business discussions, planning, and execution of the vision that drives their department.

Let's say you have six people reporting to you, and those six have five each reporting to them, and those five people collectively have seventy people reporting to them. You only have six direct reports, even though the entire chain of command reports to you. I am pointing this out because doers will manage all the way down to the seventy people in their daily jobs instead of teaching down and trusting. The challenge is to educate your direct reports to educate their direct reports and so on until that directly affects the customer, affects the product quality, or defines the job task. The hardest part of the process will be at the leadership level of the frontline leader or supervisor. Leadership should be developed at the top (your level) to evaluate whether your six direct reports do what I discuss in the next section.

DIRECT REPORTS MUST HAVE THE ABILITY TO

1. **Understand the Business of the Business:** Direct reports must understand what drives the business, the whys behind it, and the role the whys play in the business' success. They also understand the roles of their direct reports, other players, and customers in the business.

2. **Communicate:** Don't hire leaders who don't have good communication skills. If you can't communicate, you can't motivate. Knowing how and when to communicate, and how to follow up to motivate is the key to good communication. Your influence and follow-up is important to building a team. Most good leaders don't come from the formal education system; they are naturally gifted communicators.

3. **Teach Skills:** If your direct reports can't teach, it doesn't matter whether they can communicate, even if they know the business. Just because you know the business doesn't mean you can teach the business. For example, many good and great athletes, who excelled in their respective sports and are even in the Hall of Fame, have failed at coaching and teaching. It's the same in business. Just because you can do a job extremely well doesn't mean you can teach it.

4. **Plan:** To be successful, your direct reports must be able to put together a plan and strategy to execute your collaborated agreement. They must be able to make adjustments to the adjustments; only then will it be confirmed that a culture has been born to win and compete in your industry from a people and talent standpoint. Walt Disney didn't have just a vision and a plan; he also had a good training program, which has made the Disney brand so successful on a global level.

Once you have evaluated your six direct reports relative to the four skills I just mentioned, the next step is to evaluate how they develop the plan to teach the next step in the process. And the next step for them is to develop their direct reports. You will be evaluating how they are teaching and executing the next five steps covered in the next chapter: vision, goal, plan, process, and results.

Make sure you sign off on the teaching and the methods used along with the standards because you are laying the foundation to consistent results when conducting your one-on-ones with your direct reports. Your direct reports will do the same with their direct reports, and so on and so forth. The hardest job, again, will be that of the frontline leader because they have pure followers who will be doing a variety of jobs that have to be very well defined to achieve the vision and the goals that equate with the leader's success. These followers are the cash register of any business.

DEFINING BOUNDARIES

Most organizations have corporate policies, manuals, laws, rules, etc. Typically, these are included in a document or booklet that every employee is given upon being hired. The reason this resource is so important is it defines the boundaries your team needs to conform to. As the leader, it is your responsibility to instruct and encourage your team to abide by these policies. If the boundaries are not enforced, you will experience the equivalent of the Wild, Wild West. In other words, chaos is sure to ensue. It's hard to be successful without discipline. Everyone must have a vested interest in the team's success.

TREATING ALL EMPLOYEES WITH RESPECT

As we talked about earlier, it all comes down to respect. Respect basically means following the Golden Rule: Treat others the way you want to be treated. If you find out people on your team are not treating others with the same respect you give them, then at the end of the day, you need do your job—eliminate them from the team. Replace them with someone new who is coachable and understands the importance of respect.

Your goal as the leader is to provide an environment of discipline from top to bottom so all employees will know what is and is not acceptable and work as a team. Remember, all of society is represented in your workforce, and they will bring outside influences to the workforce if you do not set boundaries.

GETTING EVERYONE ON THE SAME PAGE

If you are responsible for an extremely large team, often you will have numerous direct reports who will help you manage, lead, and communicate your company's visions and goals.

To achieve this shared leadership, have more one-on-ones with your direct reports and delegate more of your leadership responsibilities to them. When you do this, you can and will experience more success and have less stress in the process. Learn to teach, and trust what you have taught. Stop being a doer!

EXERCISE

Write three ways you will include your direct reports more in the process of achieving your organization's goals.

_____

_____

_____

_____

_____

_____

_____

_____

_____

_____

_____

_____

_____

_____

_____

SUMMARY

As the leader of your team, you may not be able to execute fully everything you want, especially if your team is large. Hence, it is crucial to involve your direct reports.

The best way to involve direct reports is always to keep open lines of communication with them. Have them help you communicate boundaries to all subordinates, show respect to each other, and finally, get everyone on the same page. When you succeed at these things, you will successfully achieve the goals and visions set by your higher-ups within the organization.

CHAPTER 12

INVOLVING PEOPLE
IN THE PLAN

"Leadership is understanding people and
involving them to help you do a job."

— Arleigh Burke

"Understanding people is a mental process. You must realize
people are smart, so they know when they are being screwed.
Therefore, you must involve people in your plan."

— Isaac's Saying

In the last chapter, I discussed how important it is to involve your
direct reports in your plans. However, for the best success, you must
involve your people in the process. Share the plan, define boundaries, treat your team with respect, and get everyone on the same page.
In this chapter, I will share how to involve people to get everyone on
the same page. Failure to achieve mutual understanding will mean
failure to be successful long-term.

FIVE STEPS TO IMPROVING PROFITS THROUGH PEOPLE

Yes, I included these five steps in this book's preface, but I am repeating them here because they reflect one of the most important messages I am trying to communicate to you and your organization. Your people must engage in these five steps if you are to succeed. If you want to turn a profit and have your team members working in harmony, implement these five steps.

1. Vision

How do you see yourself being successful? How do you see your team being successful? What are you willing to accomplish? What does success look like for just your department? The vision's purpose is to encourage the leader to talk to their subordinates not as a boss but as a business partner who wants to share and compare their vision. Only after each person discusses the vision and collaborates on determining the vision can they discuss how to accomplish the vision. Every subordinate is to follow the same pattern down to the hourly worker. Once it gets to the hourly worker or the frontline person closest to the customer or production and sale of the product, the vision transforms into a job being done and very well defined.

2. Goal

How and what are you measuring for success to achieve your vision? What are you willing to accomplish? The goal must match the vision; everyone meets to align. Repeat the process above with your subordinate down to the person closest to the customer or who makes the product.

3. Plan

I encourage you to have all leaders produce a plan or plans to accomplish the vision and goal in writing. (Putting plans in writing crystalizes the goal into reality.) Most leaders enter their jobs without a plan, so they plan to fail. Be sure to include your standards and leadership style. Lead by example, define jobs, and make adjustments to the plans as needed. It's your job to communicate these plans to all leadership for teaching down. Make sure to discuss plans with your boss like you did with the vision and goal.

4. Process

The process is the start of the execution of the plans and the managing of those plans by the leaders. The process includes the Key Performance Indicators, the company policies, and the company's particular leadership style. Things will go wrong in the process. That is the part of the five steps that will test and gauge your teaching ability, help analyze your process, and allow the business to make adjustments in real time. All of these processes are vital, along with maintaining morale. What can go wrong will go wrong in the process. The process is a grind, but remember, "Repetition is the mother of all learning."

5. Results

How do you measure results from your objectives, goals, scorecard, or KPIs? (The desired results are determined in the goal and planning stage by all leaders and frontline workers.) How are we making adjustments when we are falling short of the goals? What is the plan to educate or mentor to improve results? How are you identifying performers and non-performers? How are you gauging morale and keeping it positive?

The answer is to conduct one-on-ones because it is important to make sure people don't lose sight of the vision, goal, their particular plan, and the desired results, depending on the job that was defined. Make sure you make them think! In the one-on-one, review all of the steps and follow up.

COMMUNICATING TO DIRECT REPORTS

Effective communication in an organization comes from the very top—the president, CEO, senior management, and all the C-level managers. It is their responsibility to effectively communicate to the next level of managers directly below them. They must accurately communicate the vision and goals they want to teach to the level below them. Then the mid-level managers, who just received the vision and goals, in turn, must accurately communicate to their subordinates. This communication process must occur openly and regularly all the way down to the lowest level within the organization. If, along the way, any manager fails to share the vision and goals, you will have a breakdown because everyone will not be on the same page.

GETTING ALL TO BUY IN

The goal is ultimately to have all team members buy into the vision, goals, and process. The challenge is you need to get your team to buy in with both their heads and their hands because they do the work to achieve the level of consistency you want. At the level of where the work is actually being done, no vision or goal becomes a constant reality if the frontline employee is not involved. People at this level are "the cash register" because they are where the money is made. They are closest to what you are producing and closest to your customers, so they determine your product's quality. Buy-in gives you a better chance to succeed.

Through the process, you will find out who is disrupting the process. Disruptors may not be spotted easily, so it is your goal to have solid enough relationships with your subordinates that they will help you identify those not buying into the process. But also be aware that the problem may be you; you may be exposed as an inefficient teacher, so plan on checking all the boxes before you confront a non-performer.

It is also important not to ignore good work. Don't ignore good or bad because both are an opportunity for you to teach what to do and what not to do. And continued teaching is exactly what you want to achieve. If, in the teaching process, you still aren't able to get your employee on the same page, ask questions that lead to the root cause, and then act according to what you find out. All you are looking for is effort, so as long as you can keep getting effort, keep building the relationship.

EXERCISE

List three ways you can better include your subordinates in helping you achieve your organization's vision, goals, and objectives.

_____

_____

_____

SUMMARY

At the end of the day, you must realize that whatever the product or service your company delivers to the marketplace, that is not the kind of business you are really in. To truly succeed in this marketplace, you must realize you are in the "people business." Once you realize how important it is to include all your people in the plan and you do include them, they will feel they are part of the company's plans, vision, and goals. Then they will go out of their way to support the process and help you achieve the organization's ultimate goals. When you involve your people, you will achieve success because they will all be investing in your company.

CHAPTER 13

ELIMINATING
SILOS

"Individually we are one drop but together, we are an ocean."

— Ryunosuke Satoro

"Everybody is somebody's customer, so work together."

— Isaac's Saying

Now that all your direct reports have bought into your vision for change and success, you must convince all individuals who prefer to do it their way and resist change. In this chapter, I'll explain how to deal with them and why it is so important not to overlook them.

DEFINING A SILO

I use the term "silo" to define a person or group of people who don't get along with others within the business. Often, these people come from different departments: accounting, IT, plant, sales, human resources, customer service, etc. One department always seems to be fighting with another department. Usually, it's not the departments themselves, but a silo in each department waging the war. Unfortunately, rather than realizing the silo is the problem, departments collectively turn on each other. Neither department realizes how much damage is being done to the company as a result of their perceived differences.

Leaders who enable silos are not strong enough to acknowledge others' boundaries or create their own. They will always overstep the role they were hired for, which leads to conflict. Bickering does no one any good. It only leads to bad relationships, poor employee morale, low productivity, and high turnover.

IDENTIFYING A SILO

One reason to use the five steps we discussed in Chapter 12 is because the process automatically dissolves silos through the process of creating shared visions and goals. Silos are part of human nature. Remember, the workforce is the most integrated place that most Americans go each day. After work, we usually go back to segregation, or our own silos where we are accepted and welcomed among our peers. Let's look at this situation from a cultural standpoint. In Chapter 7, we talked about diversity and how society is in your workforce. Society is conditioned to silos. For example, we silo ourselves by country, city, state, community, club, etc. We make stereotype statements like "Everyone in X city has a problem," or come up with reasons for why a community is different. All these stereotypes may not have negative connotations, yet they are in close proximity. Companies and corporations are no different, down to the department, location, shareholders, or board of directors' level. All of these people must connect after coming out of the forecast and planning sessions to execute the plan as quickly as possible. Often, those at the top don't know what the bottom is doing. In reality, the bottom is the very top of the organization because that is where the money is made.

Now back to silos. Examples of silos, as defined in the corporate world, would be: Sales doesn't like Operations and vice versa. Engineering doesn't like Maintenance and vice versa. Quality doesn't like Production. Customer Service doesn't like Marketing. You get the picture.

Silos exist because someone at the top is asleep at the wheel, so no common goal for success exists in each of the departments or silos. The first task is to define where the job task begins and ends, which eliminates all gray areas so everyone knows the boundaries along with the company policies, KPIs, and leadership styles. Second, after discussing the vision for the plan's success (follow the process in Chapter 11 for involving direct reports), sometimes the process to achieve the plan is tough to implement because of the need by those in the company's top positions to control everything. This process doesn't fit well with people who want to have control, status, or whatever drives the doers at the top.

Silos breed and grow in these environments because there is usually no accountability, and no one has clear work directions about what is considered good or acceptable. People like to know where they stand. To add further damage, doers are being promoted up the food chain into leadership roles. Doers do what they are told, which is fine, but they also don't think and plan; instead, they will show you what they think you want to see and tell you what they think you want to hear. They will fulfill a task, then wait to be told again to do it and repeat the process over and over again.

Over the last ten years, I have seen a lot of silos; in some companies, only one or two people think and the rest are doers. Let me add that I have never, ever in my life seen so many ass-kissers! Silos usually have an abundance of both. Silos don't breathe a healthy environment for good leaders to thrive in, and most people who stay in silos allow their careers to die on the vine. As a friend told me, "The further you climb the pole, the more you see the monkey's ass!" These silos will exist until a company goes out of business, merges, or sells or until someone has the balls to start thinking and implementing plans for change. Silos only exist because you have a culture of doers, not thinkers. Doers protect each other by not holding each other accountable.

Some companies survive because of their brand name, demand, little or no competition, or by generating revenue no matter how screwed up their culture is and no matter their inefficiencies and their millions of dollars of waste. Doers don't care because all they want is a paycheck. But leaders want to grow the brand, creating opportunities for the company and themselves. Sooner or later, silos will have to perform in a downturn when profit margins are squeezed, and cuts will be made in the silos that will speed up the bleeding because doers just don't know how to fix it.

To eliminate silos, leaders must have a vision and set goals that drive revenue in all departments. Then they must connect with each department head who is their internal customer and determine what success and standard operating procedures look like.

Once desired success is broken down into a goal or task form, communicate how to initiate customer satisfaction until you get to the external customer and the consumer. Hold everyone accountable based on their performance—a performance everyone was involved in planning for—and get rid of the ass-kissers because they don't think, they are lazy, and you can't trust them. You know who is doing the ass-kissing because it's your ass being kissed! Everyone else knows, so stop it! Finally, never hire anyone you can't fire.

GIVING CUSTOMERS WHAT THEY WANT

Everyone seems to think that once you give your customer what they want, the goal has been achieved. But the reality is you can give the customer what they want and still have a bad product or a product with quality issues. The customer knows what is a good or bad product. It may appear nice and shiny on the surface, but inside it may be doomed for failure. At first, the customer feels like they got what they wanted, only later to realize the product is not as good as they originally thought. Then, when the customer starts complaining, silo people start blaming everyone else instead of taking ownership for the issue as one company, one family, one vision, and fixing things to make it right and avoid future issues.

The reality is that the screw-up may have been caused by one person, but all within the organization need to take ownership for it and get it right for both that customer and future customers. This is a leadership "at the top" problem. You lead by walking around to ensure everyone is fulfilling the vision according to the process to make the customer happy.

DOING AWAY WITH "ME" MENTALITY

Another problem with silos is they are "me first" people and maybe also "you later" or "not you at all" people. This "me" mentality needs to be eliminated from within the organization. Everyone needs to take pride of ownership as one team, one unit, one family. Former US President John F. Kennedy once said in a famous speech:

> "Ask not what your country can do for you—
> ask what you can do for your country!"

I have always loved this quote, and it is so applicable to manufacturing and customer service. Everyone wants to know "What's in it for me?" instead of "What is in me for it?" When workers make this transfer of thinking, amazing visions and goals can be realized within the organization. So, as a leader, you need to recognize the silos, both on your team and on other teams, and take whatever actions are necessary to eliminate them from the process through education and accountability.

RESPECT AND GROWTH ARE CONNECTED

When people are working together and sometimes competing for the boss's attention or a raise, drama and backstabbing often become a part of the work environment. Frankly, there is no reason why you are being treated like shit and your boss doesn't know that. No reason at all! It's on your boss' watch and it reflects upon them when an employee is not treated with respect.

In weak organizations, you will often find a "mole" or "snitch" who runs to the top and tells everything, whether or not it is true. By doing so, they qualify themselves as an ass-kisser. That they can have such power means you have a weak, controlling, and non-trusting organization. I see this situation a lot in family-owned businesses. It often prevents them from experiencing real growth.

EXERCISE

Create a list of toxic, negative employees in your organization who report to you. Assist them in the next 3-6 months to achieve success by extending the olive branch and helping them set goals.

_____

_____

_____

SUMMARY

Every organization has bad apples that have risen through the ranks and are in positions of authority. Whether or not they earned their position, these people often have the worst attitude toward their job. They may be very talented, but they will blame others instead of taking ownership as a team. When this happens, it is your responsibility to act to create harmony within your team and organization.

When you eliminate the silos in your organization, you will immediately see an increase in morale, teamwork, and production. This change will lead to boosted profits that, in turn, lead to job satisfaction for all those willing to put the organization's needs in front of their own and be part of something bigger than themselves. Get on the same page, work the system, define the jobs, write the Standard Operating Procedures (SOP) manual, get input where needed, and finally inspect what you expect. As the old saying goes, "Who is watching the people who are watching the hen house?"

CHAPTER 14

KNOWING HOW
NOT TO BE A BOSS

"Leadership does not mean being bossy, always telling others what to do. No, leadership means going ahead, not putting others in the front. Good leaders lead by example. Not by decree."

— Myles Munroe

"If the fish is stinking at the tail, the head is stinking too. Some bosses walk around thinking their shit doesn't stink, but their farts give them away."

— Isaac's Saying

In the last chapter, I introduced you to the term "silos" and explained how to eliminate them before they can mess up your plans for change, growth, and implementation. In this chapter, I will discuss how *not* to be the boss everyone dislikes. Sometimes understanding how *not* to be or do something can make the difference between success and failure.

CARING ABOUT PEOPLE

The more I travel the country training, speaking, and consulting for organizations, the more HR managers tell me that "turnover" is a big issue they deal with on a regular basis. These managers consistently tell me that often when doing departing interviews with disgruntled employees, these employees are not actually quitting their jobs, but "quitting their bosses"!

To avoid this situation, as a leader, you need to care about your team, your employees. It's worth my reminding you again here of what Teddy Roosevelt said:

> "People don't care how much you know until
> they know how much you care."

Perhaps the single greatest reason your team will buy into your vision and follow you to the promised land is they know you actually care about them, their safety, their family, and most importantly, their success within the organization.

REALIZING YOU DON'T OWN THEM

As a leader, you need to realize you are not a dictator or anyone else with an elite rank. You are simply a man or a woman who has been selected because of your wisdom, knowledge, and experience to lead your subordinates to work in harmony toward achieving the organization's vision and goals.

To succeed as a leader, it's not wise to speak down, ridicule, make fun of, or punish your team. If you are to be effective in leading your team, you need to facilitate, educate, and motivate. You need to be likable and, as John Maxwell famously said:

> "To be the kind of person others want to follow."

Realize you do not own your employees. Rather, you coach them. When you operate from this mindset, you will be successful.

HAVING RESPECT FOR EMPLOYEES

If management fails to realize employees are the organization's most valuable resource, continuous quality improvement will never become a reality. The foundation for successful employee involvement is a firm belief that people want to contribute; they want to take pride in their work, and they want to feel trusted.

Everyone wants employees to have a healthier team attitude, but few leaders seem to understand their role in making it happen. Employees can't be expected to work as a team in traditional organizations that only reward people for individual performance and do not allow them to have input on how they do their jobs. Leadership is responsible for establishing an environment and structure that encourage employees to work as a team toward daily improvement. They can only do this when they have educating leaders who can communicate and motivate.

GIVING YOUR EMPLOYEES A REASON TO PERFORM

The best way to give your subordinates a reason to perform is to get them involved and encourage them to think. Then consider their advice when making your decisions. You may be surprised by just how many times employees actually have good ideas.

When you get your employees involved, they will take pride of ownership in their jobs and be more responsible in pursuing the visions and goals you have laid out for them.

Through this involvement, they will also take on leadership roles on the manufacturing floor, in the office, etc. They will buy into your vision and encourage their fellow employees to do the same.

When you accept your employees' common advice, your chances of achieving company visions and goals increase dramatically.

EXERCISE

List three ways you can be more compassionate and understanding toward your subordinates.

_____

_____

_____

_____

_____

_____

_____

_____

_____

_____

_____

_____

_____

_____

SUMMARY

As a leader, you need to remember the old KLT rule: People do business with and better perform for people whom they "know, like, and trust!" The best way to get people to like you is to listen to them, show them how much you care, and involve them in the decision-making process when you can. I will discuss this in more detail in Chapter 21 when I talk about the importance of one-on-ones.

When you realize you don't own your team, but rather, your role is to facilitate, educate, and motivate them, your team will actually respect you and perform for you. As you achieve this level of respect and admiration in your relationship with your team, high levels of achievement will occur in terms of the goals and visions set by you and your organization.

CHAPTER 15

DEFINING
JOBS

"Every child is an artist, the problem is staying
an artist when you grow up."

— Pablo Picasso

"I am not interested in how you are showing employees how it's
done. I am interested in how you are teaching employees how it's
done. I am also very interested in your strategy
and the execution of that strategy."

— Isaac's Saying

In the last chapter, I emphasized the importance of caring about your team and learning how not to be the boss many dislike. In this chapter, I will explain why it is so important to define everyone's role on the team. When everyone understands their role, amazing things can happen. When roles are not understood, complications are sure to arise with team members all pointing their fingers at one another and thinking they are not responsible for certain duties you expect them to execute.

GOOD THINGS HAPPEN WHEN EMPLOYEES UNDERSTAND

Good things happen within an organization when employees clear-ly know what is expected of them at all times. Success and failure within an organization are measured by KPIs (Key Performance Indicators), goals, tasks, or objectives.

No goal can be successful unless people at the top know how to be teachers and not doers. We discussed this concept in Chapter 13.

But the point here is that when senior management clearly communicates what is expected of their employees, good things happen because everyone is on the same page.

TRAINING EVERYONE FOR SUCCESS

Having a well-educated workforce means your organization has a clearly defined training program. That program teaches employees how to set and plan goals, and then achieve those goals by doing their jobs efficiently. However, your role as their trainer, coach, and facilitator goes even deeper.

Sometimes, you must act like your employees' mom, dad, friend, mentor, or minister. In other words, you must expose them to how to be successful in both work and life. You need to show them how to create balance in their lives and to recognize and live up to their potentials.

The bottom line: It is your responsibility to make sure you never give them a reason not to perform for you. There should be no place on your team for anyone who is not adequately trained. If and when this happens, it immediately cuts into productivity and makes for sloppy work that reduces profits.

I have a philosophy you may want to adopt: I will turn over people and terminate individuals in management before I will let go of hourly positions that are closest to our customers. More times than not, the hourly person will do a good job if the management person is the right teacher, mentor, and coach.

DEFINING ALL JOBS TOP TO BOTTOM

Virtually every company I have ever consulted for wants an educated workforce that will support the defined Standard Operating Procedures (SOP) manual. While that is the goal, it is obviously not always the reality.

If an SOP manual does not exist in your company, you need to make sure one is created sooner than later so all employees clearly know what is expected of them.

To be successful in reaching your organization's goal of improving profits through people, each and every job has to be very well defined. Most companies teach job performance responsibilities by using the longest tenured employee who does a good job, or the last hold-over from a high turnover workplace to do the training. The problem with this situation is if three different people have done the job, chances are they are teaching it three different ways. The root problem is no one is teaching from an SOP as a guideline to ensure what is being taught is being taught properly and matches or meets the safety and quality standards of the particular task. This lack of an SOP causes problems like downtime, rework, customer complaints, and inefficiencies in the process itself.

Let's talk about what I mean when I say "defining a job" and that every job in every business needs to be very well defined. I described earlier that showing employees how a job is to be done in your own way is like cooking a meal. Let's say you're making a soup, stew, or casserole; then you can add your own twist, but when it comes to baking a cake, cookies, or most desserts, you have to follow each step and measurement to the tee in order for the dessert to be perfect. Defining the jobs in your organization is similar to baking a cake, not making a stew or casserole.

First, there should be a written SOP that explains each step of the job, regardless of how many steps are in the process.

Evaluate the SOP for the end results before it goes to the customers, both internal and external, and evaluate it for quality and performance before it reaches the consumer or user.

The SOP guarantees that the product is made to perfection every time and always passes inspection, whether you are producing a product or providing customer service.

Next, a trainer's checklist should be created to ensure proper training and education in the SOP is being taught and to avoid any misunderstanding or small mishap that may lead to waste, quality problems, specification problems, bad customer service, or other inefficiencies that will bottleneck your system.

Next, there should be a train the trainer program that educates the trainer on how to teach and train from both the SOP and the trainer's checklist while evaluating and developing the talent in your organization. The education or training process should have a start time and an end time, a written and a verbal test, and a discussion before the live date when the employee begins working on their own.

As stated earlier in this book, any person with the physical and mental capabilities to do a job and who understands their job will do a good job, provided the job is very well organized and defined. However, if the job is not very well organized and defined and properly taught, management should assume they are not doing their job and act accordingly. Most of the inefficiencies, bottlenecks, and relationship problems in any organization come from top leadership's decisions or lack of decisions on how things should be done. The problem here is likely that how things are to be done is in management's heads and not on paper. Procedures need to be written down if they are to be followed completely and accurately, and the whys for following the procedures need to be clear. Just telling people how to do it over and over is not coaching and leads to the workforce being demotivated. You would be amazed by how many leaders lead that way; it tells me they are very poorly trained or not trained at all. It also tells me they are very poorly organized because they don't believe in and don't have any written plans from which to execute. And if you have met any of these types of leaders, you know they are the biggest assholes you have ever seen! They use their titles to intimidate, rather than having any education in leadership. They are the kinds of experts who are so dumb that they can't see a problem until it hits them in the face, and then they start blaming others because they don't know how to talk to people.

Okay, let me stop rambling. Sorry. They just give me the case of the red ass.

Just remember to educate your workforce. Take the time to get them involved. If you are a good teacher, good students will appear!

EXERCISE

Write out a perfect job description (if one doesn't already exist) for one of your subordinates.

_____

_____

_____

_____

_____

_____

_____

_____

_____

_____

_____

_____

_____

_____

_____

_____

_____

_____

_____

_____

_____

_____

_____

_____

_____

_____

SUMMARY

When everyone in your organization knows what is expected of them, your production will run like a finely-tuned machine.

Your job is to define the culture, set the boundaries, treat everyone with respect, and finally get them all involved. Realize your employees are the engine and you are just driving the car. They are the spokes, engine, and wheels. You are the facilitator. When everyone knows their role, the ride will be smoother.

CHAPTER 16

GETTING MOTIVATION
IN REAL LIFE

"Believe you can and you are half way there."

— Theodore Roosevelt

"It's an art to find out how to motivate people and what
to do with that motivation once you find it."

— Isaac's Saying

In the last chapter, I explained why it is so important to define everyone's roles. Now I will share with you the importance of getting your team motivated so you can achieve real results.

Motivational speaker and best-selling author Zig Ziglar said: "Of course motivation is not permanent. But then, neither is bathing; but it is something you should do on a regular basis."

STAYING FOCUSED AND POSITIVE

As the leader in your business or organization, you set the tone of the day, the structure, and the boundaries. Remember, you are the rabbit, so you set the pace.

Your influence can be a double-edged sword. On one hand, enthusiasm catches on like the common cold. On the other hand, so does negativity. If you act and think negatively, it sets a bad tone in the workplace, which leads to low productivity and morale.

Whenever I'm working with a company, I ask the leaders to find time at the start of the day to get in the right frame of mind to lead. If leaders want an enthusiastic, productive workplace, then they must generate enthusiasm from within.

Of course, we're all human. We have our bad days, both at home and at work. If you're having a bad day or just lacking enthusiasm in general, try these tips:

1. **Learn to motivate yourself from within:** Motivating from within means meditating on the good and reminding yourself why it's important for you to be an enthusiastic person. You can even go so far as to give yourself a pep talk! (I always say I talk to myself because I like talking to smart people.)

2. **Call or talk to a positive friend or mentor just to see how they are doing:** Sometimes a good, positive conversation can help you get your mind off the negative and give you a fresh point of view from which to attack your problems.

3. **Read positive books, scripture, and quotes, and think positive thoughts:** We've all heard the saying "garbage in, garbage out." That means, whatever you choose to put in your head will manifest itself in your behavior. If you only focus on the negative, you'll act negative. On the flip side, if you consume positive information and focus on the good, you'll find the motivation you're looking for.

Being a leader is not an easy job. You are responsible for motivating people with different backgrounds, personalities, histories, and more. Keep your mind fed with the right kind of motivation and enthusiasm. Build relationships. Communicate and motivate. If you do, your employees will return the favor. Remember, you get what you put out there.

GETTING PEOPLE TO DO WHAT YOU ASK

Your challenge from day one is getting people involved in pursuing and completing the goals. Ideally, you want to make them part of your goals. You want to talk to them on a business level as if they are your partners. Clearly define their roles (see Chapter 15) and make it as easy as possible for them to understand those roles and how they help to achieve the goal. When you do this, you will be amazed by how simple it is to get your team to do what you ask.

ACHIEVING WHAT YOU WANT FROM EMPLOYEES

The best way to get your employees to give you what you want is first to give them what they want. And they all want the same things: respect, explanations, an open line of communication, and to be treated equally.

Once you achieve this level in your relationship with your team, you next need to ask them what they think: How would they handle the situation? What advice do they have for you? How would they do it if they were the leader? And the question they love the most is "How do I (as your leader) improve to be both a better leader and to be more effective?" All of these questions will show them that you respect and value their opinions.

After these questions are asked, willingly and thoroughly listen to their answers and feedback. You will be amazed by how well you will be able to get productivity results from them. But remember to follow through on the advice they give you. Otherwise, people will draw their own conclusions about why you did not follow up; you always want to send the message that they are important and you listened.

HAVING THEM FOLLOW BECAUSE THEY WANT TO

Once you reach this level in your relationship with your employees, where they know and experience that you have a vested interest in their success, they will go to work for you and allow you to be their coach, mentor, and friend. They will move mountains for you when you elevate your relationship to this level. I want you to digest this thought: Don't take your job title as a leader or manager too seriously. If you do, people will feel division. Focus on being their facilitator and motivator. Coach people and they will follow you to the end of the world.

EXERCISE

List three new actions you plan to execute daily that will inspire you and your subordinates to take their job (and your job) to a higher level of production/execution.

_____

_____

_____

_____

_____

SUMMARY

At the end of the day, one reason you need to create motivation is there are no guarantees in life or in your job. Just because you are employed as a leader today does not guarantee you will hold the same job tomorrow. Your company may be sold, merged, or worst-case scenario, go out of business. Much of that is out of your control.

Therefore, I challenge you to stay motivated since you never know when it may all come to an end. Don't put all your eggs in one basket. Know how to do more than one thing, and keep setting goals.

SECTION 3

PRODUCTIVITY

"The way to get started is to quit talking and begin doing."

— Walt Disney

"Everyone has potential, but just potential will
get your ass fired. Get things done!"

— Isaac's Saying

CHAPTER 17

MANAGING KEY PERFORMANCE INDICATORS (KPIS)

"The true measure of the value of any business leader
and manager is performance."

— Brian Tracy

"Leaders must have skin in the game."

— Isaac's Saying

In the last chapter, I discussed the important of getting real about motivation. In this chapter, I will share how to implement metrics that will allow your team to have a scorecard for monitoring their progress. I will refer to this tool and/or process as "Key Performance Indicators" or KPIs.

BREAKING DOWN THE KPIS

To succeed in the manufacturing business, service business, or any business, you must put a strategic plan in place that is supported by a process. Once the plan is in place, you need to see it through. The best way to do this is to execute the plan by involving the people in the process.

Your goals need to be relative to your vision. The measuring methods are metrics that drive your bottom line. These include sales, waste, quality, and a healthy workforce. The key is to realize that the only way to succeed in all aspects of your business is by monitoring numbers or tasks.

KPIS PLAY A VITAL ROLE

KPIs are vital in any business, and they must be created at the top. They must be developed in planning sessions and passed down the chain of command.

Every KPI must have an SOP for how the job is to be done. Why? Because it determines the safety and quality of the product or service, how the product is executed or produced, and the efficiency of production or performance, and it gives people at the top an inside look at how and why their people are doing things. Also it helps with relationships because then everyone is on the same page speaking the same language.

Each department head has to be well-versed on what success means for their department. Then they must create a plan for success that involves all department workers. The right hand must know what the left hand is doing so there is no gray area and everyone has their SOP for their job.

KPIS AND EDUCATION

Frontline leaders are the most neglected leaders in many organizations because most of them come from inside the company and did good jobs as doers, but they don't understand the numbers, people, and strategy very well, and most haven't set goals in their lives and achieved them. So how do you help them become successful? That's where KPIs come in. Each job has a scorecard with their daily, weekly, or monthly goal on it that has to be performed at a high level in order to be competitive with the competition.

Education happens when leaders teach and coach how to reach goals or ask their subordinates to prepare plans to ensure daily or weekly success. When leaders lead by example and use a hands-on approach, it helps their subordinates put together mental notes and learn how to run a process. This type of coaching helps all leaders, not only the frontline ones. However, at the front level is where it has the greatest effect. Your front level worker is your cash register because they are where the money comes in. I don't believe labor is your biggest cost, but an employee in customer service who has not been trained on how to manage people and product sends a negative vibe to some customers that can ultimately cost you business and affect your bottom line.

Furthermore, having an inefficient leader of a process leads to quality problems, labor problems, downtime, etc.—all of which hurt the bottom line. Teaching and mentoring on the KPIs is the best way to train frontline leaders. The problem is there are very few teachers out there, and most leadership teams are made up from people who came through the formal education system or doers, neither of whom have yet worked from the top to the bottom, or the bottom to the top, and most of them cannot teach. Teaching and mentoring some people on the KPIs takes time and patience, and to be successful, teaching should be detailed. That means putting employees in every situation possible and coaching them through the good, the bad, and the ugly, meaning the process and the people.

Until KPI education is invested in, most companies will be wasting time and money on some fancy coach selling them tools of continued improvement. Very few of these coaches will show you how to do it on the floor or in real time or will understand what the leader goes through daily. They are selling tools, and tools are no good to people who haven't been trained on how to use them. You have to learn from on-the-job-training before knowing how to do what or with which tool. Know how to analyze your process and people. For example, a doctor, brick mason, and chemist may all be good at what they do mentally and physically. The tools help them do it with ease. Do you get the point? Get the right people on the bus and build a strong foundation.

A SAMPLE KPI SHEET

As mentioned above, Standard Operating Procedures (SOP) are vital to producing the correct KPIs. Each job has to be performed in a certain way for it to be perfect. The steps for how you do a job or task must be taught; then successful performance of the task or job becomes the true measurement of success for whatever product or service you sell; in other words, the SOPs are turned into KPIs. When teaching, every step of the SOP should be taught to the people actually doing the job. When people understand their jobs, they will do good jobs. If they don't understand their jobs, you must assume leadership is not doing their job, and leadership must act accordingly. Every job in your company must have an SOP to be measured by a KPI. For example, the SOP indicates that a job should be done a certain way to produce its desired outcome. Following the SOP specs ensures the KPIs are correct, which connects the organization's top to its bottom.

As a leader, educating your team on KPIs is the lifeblood of your success. Your job, as stated before, is to develop talent. Leaders have to focus on the process and be able to read processes in real time on multiple fronts. Then they must marry their people to the process with the people's input, all while creating motivation and confidence. Go through your processes; have your one-on-ones to mentor your team, instill trust in them, and teach them to be just as good as or better than you. Everyone needs a mentor to break down the process; workers will need to learn the system before they can manage the system; lead by example and put forth the effort to educate and mentor. Good luck!

EXERCISE

What three key measurements will you add to your team on a daily basis to achieve even better results?

_____

_____

_____

SUMMARY

My friend Patrick Snow always uses this quote, which I feel is applicable for everything from weight loss to wealth building:

"You cannot improve what you don't measure!"

It is so true and illustrates the main point I am trying to communicate in this chapter. If you do not have a KPI program in place, I challenge you to get one started before you finish reading this book.

CHAPTER 18

BALANCING LIFE
AND WORK

"You will never feel truly satisfied by work
until you are satisfied by life."

— Heather Schuck

"Do what you love and you will find your purpose in life."

— Isaac's Saying

In the last chapter, I introduced you to the measuring concept of Key Performance Indicators. In this chapter, I will encourage you to create a healthy balance between life and work, both to take time off as needed and to invest in your employees. We will discuss numerous character traits you can develop and build on, not only to make you more valuable to your organization, but so you can be a more valuable asset to yourself, your friends, and your family.

I strongly recommend you review all of the character traits discussed in this chapter with all of your subordinates. Encourage them to work on themselves in these areas, and you do the same. By doing so, you will quickly see your employees will be engaged in working on themselves and the company visions; as a result, they will be happier and will produce healthier profits for the company.

OVERCOMING PROBLEMS

Everyone faces problems. It is just a given. However, the difference between success and failure often boils down to meeting those obstacles head-on to overcome them. When faced with courage and confidence, problems that might seem like mountains can be turned into smaller problems and leveled, one molehill at a time. As each molehill crumbles, you find yourself stronger, more courageous, and more confident in your abilities.

BUILDING CONFIDENCE

Confidence in yourself—in what you do and the tools you use—is an important part of any successful career. Build your confidence now and it will pay off sooner than you think. One of the best ways to build confidence is to pursue opportunities one at a time. Each achievement will then boost your confidence.

A great difference exists between a bragging, loud person and a quiet, confident person. True confidence comes only from experience and knowledge, recognizing that you have the ability to do what you must. Confidence only comes to those who will study and practice. By acting too confident, without knowledge or experience, you will make yourself look ridiculous. You don't have to tell people how good you are. Show them with confidence and they will respect you.

Confidence in yourself makes other people confident in you. It makes them cooperate with you and be enthusiastic about you and your abilities. Confidence gives you poise, balance, and steadiness.

The industrialist Andrew Carnegie once said, "Immense power is acquired by assuring yourself in your secret reveries that you were born to control affairs."

AVOIDING IMPATIENCE

The old saying "Patience is a virtue" is as true today as when it was first spoken. Sometimes, in a rush to get things done, you may lose patience with things, people, and yourself. Instead of making the situation better, your impatience makes things worse.

Losing patience—allowing frustration to anger or cloud your thinking—does no one any good. Impatience can make what might otherwise be obvious answers impossible to see, and it can make other people not want to be around you. Be patient with things you can't control, and with those you can. Patience can help you recognize the difference between the two.

BEING UNSELFISH

Are you always looking out for number one? Do you figure the squeaky wheel gets the most grease? You might be right in the short-term, but what about in the long-term?

The human instinct for survival is strong, but you differ from animals because you're able to temper that instinct with intelligence. You are able to recognize it is often in your own best interest to put others ahead of yourself—to put the needs of your organization, team, family, etc. ahead of your own desires. The selfish person will usually lose more than they will gain. They'll lose the trust and respect of other people.

KNOWING YOURSELF AND UNDERSTANDING OTHERS

Did you ever listen to a recording of yourself and think, "Hey, that doesn't sound anything like me?" Your friends, however, immediately recognized the voice as yours.

Just as you fail to know how you sound to other people, you don't always know how others see you and judge your actions. Of course, you can never see yourself exactly as others do. How your actions are interpreted depends on the other person's values, expectations, and past experiences. But you can still get a fairly accurate picture of yourself if you honestly and objectively rate yourself on a regular basis. A simple way to do this is to imagine yourself as a complete stranger, and then try to look at yourself as others see you.

In the same way, you can better understand the actions of others if you put yourself in their shoes for a while. Again, you can't know exactly how another person thinks, but this approach will often allow you to better appreciate another person's position and attitudes.

"Know thyself" is an age-old saying that still rings true. Understanding yourself is the first step in better understanding others.

BUILDING TRUST

Nothing grows faster than a lie. Lies feed on themselves because when one lie is told, another must soon follow to support it. If the truth sometimes hurts, the pain is slight compared to the harm caused by a pack of lies.

Lying can become a habit, and some people fall into the habit so easily they can't tell the difference between honesty and a lie. They live with their lies so long they come to believe them, even if no one else does. They don't know what they don't know.

A lie, no matter how well it has been built, will always be discovered, sooner or later. When it is discovered, the outcome will be even worse than what the liar was trying to hide in the first place. Like the boy who cried wolf, it will be a long time before people will be able to trust the liar again. People are always reluctant to place trust in someone who has been less than honest with them. Trustworthiness is a delicate quality that takes a long time to build, but it can be destroyed with a single lie.

You should make it easy for people to depend on you by fulfilling obligations and promises you make, doing what you say you will do, and being honest in your relationships with others and with yourself. Results depend on relationships.

THINKING SAFETY

You are responsible, to some degree, for the safety of yourself and others. That's because accidents don't just happen. They are caused by people doing something they shouldn't, or not doing something they should. Yes, physical conditions add to accidents, but it takes people's behavior combined with these hazards to result in accidents and injuries.

By having a positive attitude toward safety, by thinking safe and acting safe, you can go a long way toward stopping accidents.

First, within your organization or manufacturing floor, learn to recognize possible accident-causing situations. Failure to see the possibility of danger is a major factor behind many accidents. Second, take appropriate action to avoid dangerous situations. Take time to think about safe ways to do a job. In other words, be careful when you see a potential safety risk. And third, take an active part in preventing accidents by addressing an unsafe condition or stopping a hazard from continuing needlessly.

Always establish a habit of "safe thinking" and it will become natural for you to do things correctly and safely.

ORGANIZATION

Well-organized people are better able to work toward productivity, quality, and plant safety than disorganized employees. It is important to follow simple organizational guidelines so time can be used to its fullest instead of being wasted.

Tools, equipment, paperwork, and other items should all be kept in specific places. This designation does away with lost time spent looking for misplaced items. Return all items to their proper places when finished using them. Here is an example:

Mark, a friend of mine, is a director of operations. He was doing a walk-through in his plant when he saw some hoses sprawled across the floor that posed a tripping hazard. He asked the department leader to make sure the hoses were put back in place. The next day while inspecting the same area, he saw the same thing. The department leader, when questioned, rebutted that the employee wasn't finished using them. (That made me laugh so hard along with my friend.) Mark said, "Look; it is simple. When you finish, put the hose back where you found it, and don't wander off and leave it on the floor. Finish the job." It's that simple; just put the hose back. My question to you is: What hoses or other potentially dangerous equipment do you have on your manufacturing floor waiting for an accident to happen? Are there other tripping hazards in the office or places within your work area?

Stick to procedures. Once you decide on a good system of organization, don't change it—unless you find a better way. One-on-ones with your team will help you find better ways.

Don't let unnecessary materials pile up. Store materials when you aren't using them, and get rid of material when you know you won't use it. Always keep maintenance in mind. Routinely maintain your organization system, and make sure things are properly organized. Inspect what you expect.

IMPLEMENTING MENTAL HEALTH DAYS

Sometimes you need to give yourself time away from your job, away from the pressures of daily life, to recharge your batteries. When you do so, you will be in a better position to deliver when you are called upon. It is human nature to have good days and bad days and sometimes not to have the drive to produce.

Whenever I am up against the clock and faced with a deadline or a responsibility, I recite this phrase that helps me realize it is go time: "Come on, baby; you got to go!" This works for me, so I am asking you to find out what works for you. Maybe it is prayer, meditation, fishing, yoga, running, biking, taking a vacation, or exercising. Whatever it is, you need to find it and allow that activity to recharge your battery so you can get back in the game. I don't believe in overworking, just under-recuperating.

I also suggest you invest one hour per day at work to recharge your batteries. Perhaps this is reading industry journals to learn more about your industry; maybe it is taking ownership of your lunch hour and going for an hour-long walk. The beautiful thing about this strategy is it is a way to get better and nourish your soul without actually taking time off from work.

Once you have figured out how to stay motivated, openly discuss these strategies and techniques with your team because, chances are, if you are going through stressful times, then so are your team members. See if you can score your own motivation daily on a scale of 1-10 with 10 being the highest. Then ask your team to do the same for themselves. Try to identify what days of the week your scores are consistently low, and see if you can identify outside forces that are keeping your numbers down at certain times. The biggest thing I want you to take away from this section (and this chapter) is you must not rely on other people to keep you motivated; motivation must be something you learn to do internally for yourself. Once you learn to motivate yourself internally, you will always be in a position to live a balanced life between life and work. It starts with having a passion to achieve something.

EXERCISE

List three new changes to both your work and your life that you will begin implementing immediately to give you more balance.

_____

_____

_____

_____

_____

_____

SUMMARY

There is an old saying that goes: "You can't pour from an empty cup."

Staying motivated and achieving balance between life and work will always be one of your greatest challenges. I challenge you to find that exercise, routine, prayer, or spiritual practice that will keep you centered. When you find it, practice it daily; it will allow you to become an even better leader for your team. Then work within your team to help them also find their balance. When you succeed at this, you will have a healthy workforce, and a healthy workforce leads to healthy profits through motivated people, people who have a goal and a purpose. People do what their culture allows them to.

CHAPTER 19

FOCUSING
ON QUALITY

"No one knows the cost of a defective product—don't tell me you do. You know the cost of replacing it, but not the cost of a dissatisfied customer."

— W. Edwards Deming

"Bad quality is like waking up to your favorite cereal to find there is no milk."

— Isaac's Saying

In the last chapter, I encouraged you to balance life and work (not only for you, but also for your team. In this chapter, I will share with you a multitude of ways you and your organization can focus on delivering quality products and services to your customers, not only to make them happy clients, but also so they will refer others to you and your organization for years to come. I attribute much of what I learned about quality from one of my mentors, George Howard.

THE ARRIVAL OF QUALITY MANAGEMENT

The primary emphasis in business, especially manufacturing, has been productivity. This translates into an emphasis on quality, while meeting minimal quality standards. The emphasis on product design has been driven by technology and cosmetic features. This approach worked quite well, as long as it was the approach of all the players in the market.

However, as a result of competition and the development of a world economy, the emphasis has now changed to quality. The quality management approach provides a viewpoint for a more effective use of technology in both internal processes and products, while maintaining the cosmetic features desired by the customer. At the same time, the highest standards of quality are maintained and continuously improved while reducing the cost of production. The design of a product is driven by customer satisfaction criteria rather than technology.

While most admit that this approach is just good common sense, it is also revolutionary. It usually takes several years of searching for the "quick fix" to finally realize that producing the highest quality at competitive prices requires a total organizational culture change. This way of doing business influences every decision, every day, and requires a long-term commitment to the principles of quality management.

THE ORIGINS OF QUALITY MANAGEMENT

Until recently, most quality management initiatives started as an attempt to survive adversity. The Japanese economy was devastated after World War II, and the industry that existed could not compete in foreign markets because of poor quality. As a result, according to quality management gurus Dr. J. M. Juran and Dr. W. Edwards Deming, the Japanese came to understand that emphasis on quality would naturally result in higher productivity and reduced costs.[2]

---

2. https://www.juran.com/blog/the-history-of-quality/. Accessed July 1, 2021.

Because Japan improved the quality of its products, those products became competitive on the world stage. The adversity caused in the United States by Japanese competition meant the American automotive industry was finally forced to recognize the benefits of quality management. Other American companies then began adopting quality management practices due to pressure from customers and domestic competition.

In 1987, Congress established the Malcolm Baldridge National Quality Award to recognize US companies that excel in quality achievement and quality management. The award was first presented in 1988. This award, and the ISO 9000 family of quality management system designed to meet statutory and regulatory requirements related to a product or service, are still the benchmark for quality all these years later.

Companies leading the way in quality improvement are constantly looking for new means of maintaining contact with the customer and letting the customer know they sincerely want customer feedback. Regular meetings with business customers and visits to their facilities to see first-hand how your product is being used will establish the business partner relationships needed to continuously improve customer satisfaction.

Satisfying customers is the only reason you are in business. The whole objective of the techniques and concepts presented in this book is to provide the means to establish a system for continuously improving your ability to satisfy your customer. All intermediate and long-term organizational planning must be shaped by that end goal. You can only do that by educating the workforce.

CONTINUOUS IMPROVEMENT

Focus on the continuous quality improvement of an organization's products and services must permeate every facet of that organization. Essentially, it means no product, process, or any other aspect of the organization is ever good enough. Room for improvement always exists, and the company objective is to challenge itself daily to improve.

Continuous improvement, as it relates to systems problems, is a pro-active approach rather than the reactive, firefighting one so common in today's work world. Putting out fires does not improve the product or system; it only maintains the status quo. True improvement happens when the cause of the fire is eliminated and is allowed no opportunity to recur. This situation applies to all systems in the organization.

Continuous improvement does not end, even if perfection is achieved in meeting product specifications. It means going beyond that goal. Even a product that meets the specifications varies to some degree from absolute perfection. The goal must be continuously to work toward reducing the variation. True perfection is a wholly perfect product. Minimize the variables and increase efficiencies.

In a society accustomed to tangible numerical goals that define what is "good enough," the ongoing nature of the continuous improvement goal may at first seems demotivating. However, the opportunity to participate in constantly achieving new standards of excellence is a very motivating experience. Moreover, it is the only way to compete.

Inherent in the concept of continuous improvement is long-term planning and decision-making. Transitioning from a traditional short-term rationale designed to meet quarterly or annual performance expectations to decisions that will not bear fruit for 2-5 years may be the most difficult adjustment top management must make. Continuous improvement will require short-term sacrifices and patience to stay the course. And remember, you must involve the people who do the work to improve profits.

IMPROVING SUPERVISION

Continuous improvement requires that supervision be improved at all levels in the organization. Supervisors need to spend time helping their people do a better job. They must become teachers and coaches who support their employees and take action to remove any obstacles to quality work. Supervisors and managers must lead the way in tearing down barriers between functions and silos while establishing the internal customer relationships that allow the whole organization to become a team. Essentially, they must become leaders rather than managers of people. You manage inventory; you lead people.

Dr. W. Edward Deming's eighth point of management obligations is "drive out fear so that everyone can work effectively for the company." In most companies, employees are afraid to disagree with the boss, propose new ideas, ask questions, or admit mistakes. In such cases, most workers and managers do not understand what their jobs are and they are afraid to ask. An environment must be created in which people are encouraged to ask questions, make suggestions, and report trouble. In general, the fears that restrict upward communication need to be driven out. Covering my five steps from Chapter 12 and having one-on-ones improve your chances of doing just that.

Upper management also has fears that restrict the downward flow of information, which would promote employee involvement. These fears include the fear of losing control and the fear of failure, both of which are based on a lack of trust in people. Employee involvement means asking people to accept more responsibility for something over which they have no control. Employee involvement also means asking people to be more concerned about the business' wellbeing. This is impossible if the employees have no understanding of the organization's overall wellbeing. Employee involvement also increases the flow of upward communication. But if there is no response from upper management, there is no incentive for upward communication flow. To encourage this flow and participation, four requirements must be in place:

1. The Brain Line Must Be Destroyed.

Traditional management practices seem to have been based on the theory that below a certain level or line in the organization, people do not have brains. At least they have not been allowed to use them. Even though management must assume responsibility for implementing systems of improvements, it must be recognized that supervisors and employees at the lower levels can provide input for the requirements that must be made. I call lower levels the cash register. It is where the money is made, so it only makes sense to involve these people.

2. People Must Be Allowed to Take Pride in Their Work.

Some managers seem to think pride of workmanship is an attitude workers should bring to the job regardless of the situation. Most people want to take pride in their work, but they cannot if there are poor systems, poor materials to work with, equipment that does not function properly, equipment that breaks down, a lack of proper tools, ineffective supervision, and no one who will listen to their problems. Management must realize that poor employee attitudes are largely the result of employees' healthy concern for doing their job well and being unable to do so. If leadership won't listen, a union will.

3. Mistakes and Problems Must Be Viewed As an Opportunity to Learn (Rather Than as Someone's Fault).

Many problems are never uncovered due to an employee's reluctance to reveal them. Traditionally, management tends to place blame on people as a way of dealing with problems. The effective way to eliminate problems is to attack the problems, not the people. If the cause for most of these problems is properly placed on the system, then the way is cleared to discover solutions. Also, it must be recognized that mistakes will be made in trying to improve systems. These mistakes should be controlled, but tolerated, if change is to occur. Mistakes happen; that's why pencils have erasers.

4. Management Must Be Responsible for Improvement.

To improve productivity, you must recognize that management, rather than employees doing the work, are responsible for 80-85 percent of the problems within an organization. Therefore, management must carry the primary responsibility for making quality improvement a way of life.

Most of the problems that occur are inherent within the "systems" in the company. These systems are controlled by, and can only be changed by, management. Such systems are the result of policies, procedures, methods, capital equipment, and behavior rewards found within the company.

A classic example of the type of system problems that must be identified and eliminated occurred during the early stages of quality improvement implementation at an Automotive Operations Division of Rockwell International. A plant manager, seeking to find out why quality improvement at his plant had stalled, decided to personally chart performance on a particular machine. His goal was to show operators his personal commitment to improvement, but he found a few surprises in his experiment. It was not employee attitude or work habits that were hindering progress. Instead, the plant manager found the following obstacles to improvement:

1. He could not get the inspection gauge to work properly.

2. He took the gauge to the tool crib to try to replace the part on it, but found the crib had been out of those and many other spare parts for months due to budget cutbacks.

3. Upon returning to the machine, he found it needed maintenance.

4. In addition, the machine was operating in such a way that chips continued to jam it, leading to further delays.

It seems, all in all, he learned very little about control charting, but instead experienced firsthand the environment he had created by his own management actions.

The amount and rate of improvement is dependent on leadership provided by management. Management's philosophy about people must be one that leads to the removal of barriers between employees at all levels and creates incentives for employee participation. The energy and knowledge of the organization's people must be unleashed for the tools for continuous improvement to be beneficial. People will get better based on what they have been taught.

THE FOUR STAGES OF WORLD-CLASS QUALITY

World-class quality will not be achieved overnight. Its evolution has four natural stages. To reach stage four, you must first begin the journey.

EVOLUTION TO WORLD CLASS

	STAGE 1	STAGE 2	STAGE 3	STAGE 4
CHARACTERISTICS	DETECTION	PREVENTION	QUALITY ASSURANCE	WORLD CLASS
VIEW OF QUALITY	PROBLEM TO BE SOLVED	PROBLEM TO BE SOLVED	PROACTIVE PROBLEM SOLVING	COMPETITIVE OPPORTUNITY
EMPHASIS	PRODUCT UNIFORMITY	UNIFORMITY - LESS INSPECTION	ALL FUNCTIONS PREVENTING FAILURES	MARKET & CUSTOMER NEEDS
METHODS	GAUGING & MEASUREMENT	SPC	PROGRAMS & SYSTEMS	STRATEGIC PLANNING
ROLE OF QUALITY DEPARTMENT	INSPECTION, SORTING & GRADING	PREVENTION, APPLYING SPC	QUALITY MEASUREMENT, PLANNING, DESIGN	GOAL-SETTING, TRAINING, CONSULTING, PROGRAM DESIGN
RESPONSIBILITY OF QUALITY	QUALITY DEPARTMENT	MANUFACTURING & ENGINEERING	ALL DEPARTMENTS	ALL WITH STRONG TOP MGMT. LEADERSHIP
APPROACH	INSPECT IN QUALITY	QUALITY IN CONTROL	BUILD IN CONTROL	MANAGE IN CONTROL

TOTAL QUALITY CONTROL (TQC)

What is new about the idea of controlling quality? Yes, companies have devoted people and procedures to quality control for years. The problem is those methods have resulted in an inefficient control of quality. The approach has been to concentrate on quality and sort out the defects at the end of the process. True control of quality involves reduction in the number of defects by eliminating their causes. It also means emphasis on controlling and adding the quality characteristics that result in customer satisfaction.

Achieving Total Quality Control (TQC) requires more than just learning new techniques for monitoring quality. It also involves an attitude about quality that motivates the most effective use of the techniques.

Three principles of the TQC attitude are:

1. Defect-free output is more important than output itself.

2. Defects, errors, and breakdowns can be prevented.

3. Prevention is cheaper than rework.

DEFINITION OF QUALITY

Total Quality Control begins with a new and expanded definition of quality and its control. American industry has defined product quality only in terms of end product or service. A common assumption has been that an increase in product quality normally means an increase in production cost. Using the traditional approaches and definitions of quality improvement, that assumption has been true since the emphasis has been on detection rather than protection.

TQC views on quality are:

1. Higher quality materials often reduce total cost because they are less expensive to use in the process.

2. Less variability (tighter specs) at a lower cost due to improved design and production methods.

3. Increased product options.

4. Higher technology but simpler-to-use product.

5. Higher technology equipment is appropriately used in simpler manufacturing methods.

6. Operator responsibility for quality to prevent defects.

7. Quality as defined by the customer.

Even the definition of the end product's quality has been off target. It must be redefined with an emphasis on customer orientation rather than the company determining engineering standards or specifications. This means using customer terminology to define quality rather than only raw material standards, tolerance limits, or chemical analysis. For example, the consumer wants a car that has a good style, is a comfortable ride, has good acceleration, and is dependable and safe. The engineering standards that reflect these requirements are the important ones. Being customer-oriented means emphasizing product benefits over features. Features tell what a product is; benefits describe what it will do for the customer.

The *Juran Quality Control Handbook* by Joseph Juran and Joseph Defeo provides multiple means for product quality with the two most dominant being: 1) "Product features which meet the needs of customers and thereby provide product satisfaction" and 2) "Freedom from deficiencies." Juran and Defeo also define quality as "Fitness for use" with the parameters being availability, reliability, maintainability, and manufacturability.

Quality cannot be rationally defined without consideration of price and quality. Quality improvements that result in an overpriced product and not enough quality will result in customer dissatisfaction. In his book, *What Is Total Quality Control?*, Kaouru Ishikawa writes: "The definition of quality must also be expanded beyond the end product to include the quality of work, service, systems, process, people, objectives and company. Improvements in these areas will allow for increased product quality while controlling or reducing costs and improving productivity."

In *Building a Chain of Customers*, Richard Schonberger lists twelve dimensions of quality:

1.   Conformance to specifications

2.   Performance (Surveys reveal that performance is the number one way consumers think about quality.)

3.   Quick response (the time to respond to the customer request)

4.   Quick-change expertise (ability to change product mix to meet customer demand)

5.   Features

6.   Reliability (failure-free operation over time)

7.   Durability

8.   Serviceability (ease of servicing goods)

9.   Aesthetics (factors that appeal to the eye or other senses)

10. Perceived quality (reputation, brand loyalty)

11. Humanity (services or goods with the right human touch)

12. Value (how much of the other dimensions we get for the price)

TIME IS QUALITY FACTOR

Items three and four on Schonberger's list introduce time as a factor in quality. Time has been overlooked not only as a quality factor but also as a cost factor. The definition of item twelve, value, indicates the cost must also be considered in defining quality. A proper understanding of how time is both a quality and a cost factor will help us understand why quality must become the primary concern of every function in the organization.

Shortened product development and manufacturing lead times improve your ability to provide the right products in the right amounts at the right time. Using project teams that include representatives from marketing, product engineering, manufacturing, purchasing, and other functions directly affected in getting the product to the customer dramatically shortens product development and improves efficiency for any manufacturing support function, which in turn normally decreases manufacturing lead-time. Just-In-Time (JIT) production not only relies on quality but also improves quality. (JIT means producing a quality product and shipping it to the customer without storing it.)

CONCEPTS OF QUALITY

It may be more appropriate to refer to the concept of quality than the definition because all of these ideas are relevant to the view of quality required to be competitive in today's world. The goal should be quality that will not only make you first in sales, but also the customer's first choice. There is a difference. Price slashing could make you feel first in sales only—quality will make you first in choice.

CONTINUOUS IMPROVEMENT OF QUALITY

The goal of continuously improving quality is primarily achieved by continuously improving your systems that determine the quality of your product or service. The systems within an organization are those policies, procedures, and methods for accomplishing work. Included in those are the raw materials, equipment, paper forms, software, and tools used. These systems may be the manufacturing process or a segment of it, policies and procedures for purchasing materials, inspection materials, accounting methods, engineering design methods, or the routing of a piece of paper.

Most problems with any organization are due to problems within these systems. For example, a product shipment may be late due to an equipment breakdown in production, or a drill press machine may start producing defective parts due to a worn drill bit. Billing errors in accounting may be the result of poor procedures or a form that is confusing to the clerks. These are problems inherent in the system and not the fault of the person. Only management has the authority to change these systems; therefore, they are responsible for these problems. Even many problems that may be blamed on people are actually the result of poor or no training, which is also the responsibility of management. This idea must be accepted before improvement can be made because problems can't be eliminated without proper assignment of their causes.

The continuous search to eliminate the causes of variation goes beyond a "managing by specification" approach, which is encouraged by such concepts as Zero Defects. The goal of Zero Defects is for all products to meet specifications. Even though it seems to be a worthy goal, you must discontinue the practice of managing by specifications. The continuous elimination of the causes of variation will lead you to continue to improve the quality of the product that meets specifications and will allow specifications to be moved closer to perfection.

The key to Total Quality Control is the goal of continuous improvement of the systems, as well as the product features that produce customer satisfaction and customer service.

ERROR PREVENTION

The purpose of continuously improving your system is to find ways to prevent errors rather than apply temporary quick fixes to get you through the day. Without some permanent change in the system, these problems will continue to occur. The three principles of the TQC attitude previously mentioned are essential to error prevention.

Error and defect prevention are achieved when you make it at least as easy to do the job right as to do the job wrong. People will always choose to do it right under those conditions. Mistakes are made when it is easier to do it wrong.

One primary reason quality has always been more expensive is the emphasis has been on defect detention rather than prevention. If you tighten specifications in order to improve quality without improving the capability of your process, then cost automatically rises. Tightened specifications will mean a higher defect rate, which increases rework and scrap rates. These tightened specifications usually lead to increased inspection, as if you can inspect quality into the product. Increased inspection also leads to more cost. It is easy to find many ingenious ways to add cost to our process.

The focus of Total Quality Control is improving your process in a way that prevents defects and allows you to do the work right the first time. Quality is built into the product, not inspected in. Rather than putting out fires, you are preventing them. Of course, this requires the provocative long-term approach to running your business rather than the traditional reactive short-term approach. It requires spending money now to save money later. It may mean sacrificing production today by shutting down equipment for preventative maintenance or repairing a breakdown properly to prevent more problems down the road. It means allowing employees time away from production to participate in problem-solving (error-prevention) meetings. It means listening to those who know most about the problems—those who actually do the work.

Interpretation of preventative problem recurrence can be deceiving. One such misinterpretation occurred with a device attached to a machine by four bolts. Bolt number one often snapped, so it was replaced by a larger bolt. When the second bolt gave problems, all four bolts were replaced with larger bolts. Then the iron plate used as a holder broke in half and was subsequently replaced with a thicker plate. Is this recurrence prevention? No. Further study revealed that the vibration was the cause of the problem, so that was eliminated. Still, was this cause prevention? No. Why was the vibration not detected during the testing of the product? Test procedures must be reevaluated before recurrence can be prevented.

TRANSFERRING RESPONSIBILITY FOR QUALITY

Continuous improvement through error prevention is essentially a never-ending search for better ways to do the job right the first time. Achieving this goal will require placing the responsibility for quality in the hands of the workers who have direct control over how the job is done the first time. Unless this is done, your ability to improve will be severely limited, so get your people involved.

You have always wanted your workers who have the most direct effect on quality to be concerned about quality, yet most companies have structured their organization and job responsibilities in a way that conflicts with this objective. The president of a company well-known for quality said that quality comes from the heads and hearts of his employees. However, most managers have not allowed or caused people to put their heads and hearts into their jobs. Management may talk about the need for quality and criticize workers for the poor quality of their products, but upper-level actions have indicated that management's true priority is meeting production quotas, regardless of quality. Therefore, the workers' ability to control the quality of work they do is limited.

The responsibility of quality must be formally transferred from the Quality Control department to the production worker. To make this happen, you must give the worker the ability to control and verify quality. This means providing them with a better understanding of the "what" and "why" about quality as it relates to their jobs. It means having employees check the quality of their work and maintain statistical control charts on their operation. It means listening to them about how to improve the process. Essentially, it means recognizing these workers as the functional experts they truly are.

Achieving Total Quality Control requires that the quality control department's function changes from one of being totally responsible. This change in job definition is not so much a change in QC's job functions as it is an adjustment in better defining what the job has been all along. QC has never been able to direct control quality—only the worker can do this. This misplacement of responsibility has produced a situation where no one is able to control quality.

If changes are not made to QC, the cost of the lack of quality can be astronomical. Due to a lack of true commitment, most organizations have no idea how much it is costing them to put out fires rather than prevent them. That is what Deming was talking about in the quote that kicked off this chapter. One way to determine that cost is by computing the cost of quality. In fact, it should be one of the first things accomplished in the implementation of Total Quality Control. The figures will provide you with a basis for setting TQC goals and allow you to measure progress toward those goals. Also, computing the cost will most likely increase your motivation to implement TQC once you determine the true cost of quality and see how much room for improvement exists.

Studies made in this area indicate that white-collar workers are spending 20-35 percent of their time either checking to ensure output is correct or redoing incorrect output. The total costs of quality may run as high as 50 percent of the sales price. What this should be may vary according to the product, but quality experts say anything over 8 percent should be considered excessive. A goal should be to reduce it to below 5 percent.

STATISTICAL METHODS OF CONTROLLING AND IMPROVING QUALITY

The use of statistics in monitoring and improving organizational systems was pioneered by the Japanese applications of Dr. Deming and Dr. Juran's teaching in the early 1950s. Everyone in the organization needs to understand how to use at least some of these tools.

Before a manager can use these tools effectively, they need to understand the three most important elements of the manufacturing process:

1. The Production Process

2. Its Output

3. The Variables (that affect process, output, and people)

The production process involves the total input of people, equipment, materials, method, and environment.

Output is the goods and services produced. Quality can be maintained if significant and frequent data is available to prove the product is being produced. Quality can be maintained if significant and frequent data is available to prove the product is being produced according to the specified standards. The collected data will indicate where the changes are needed—in an area of the process, an aspect of the output, or both.

Variability, the third element, is the very essence of nature; like snowflakes, no two are ever alike. This is essentially true of man-made objects.

VARIATION

Understanding statistics begins with understanding variation. Data collected on any problems, series of events, or manufacturing situation will always exhibit variation. Instead of being exactly the same, from time to time or point to point, the numbers will vary. Essentially, it is normal to expect a certain amount of variation in any system. You can never produce two items that are exactly the same.

A common way of attempting to control this variation is by setting engineering standards in the form of acceptable tolerance limits. In a drilling operation on a wood block, the nominal dimensions may be a 1" hole, but the tolerance limits may allow for a variation of 0.1" above or below 1". Anything falling between 0.9" and 1.1" is acceptable. These tolerance limits are set because it is recognized that no system can produce perfect 1" holes every time. In fact, most of the diameters will fall somewhere above or below the nominal dimension. This is true of any system, whether it is a drilling operation or an accounting procedure.

Causes of variation are categorized as either common (natural or system) or special (assignable or operational). Statistical Process Control is a feedback system that tells you whether the variation in the output is due to common or special causes.

Common causes occur randomly during the operation process, and they can't be isolated as unique, definable causes. The extent of common causes should always fall within a normal curve of distribution on an SPC graph or chart. They are expressions of the natural variation embodied in the process according to the laws of chance.

The only way to reduce variation stemming from common cause is to physically change the process itself. Correction of defects resulting from common causes could come from such things as increasing technical precision, better control of materials used, refinements in the description of operating procedures, and improvement in environmental factors.

Since processes are mainly controlled by management, it is up to them to make the necessary changes to correct problems resulting from common causes. However, since the frontline workers are closer to the process, they are in a good position to identify common causes and bring them to management's attention, if they like management. If they don't and you didn't engage them from the beginning, you will have a long road ahead of you. Remember, profits are realized through people.

Special causes of variation are those not inherent in the system but that occur as a result of operating the system. These causes are usually related to operator skill, source of materials used, the procedures followed, the condition of the machines, or the environment. Measurement errors also fall into the category of special causes. These errors can greatly mislead us into auditing the process. It is essential that measurements are done without bias and procedures are verified for consistency.

The Japanese feel any variation from the nominal value result is a loss and results in their constant striving to reduce. They understand the loss of quality when an undersized shaft is matched with an oversized hole or vice versa. Even though both products meet the specifications and will function, operability and durability are reduced. Thus, the greater the variation is from the nominal value, the greater the loss of quality.

The ability to produce superior products is based on the goal of continuously decreasing output variation by continuously improving the systems. The Japanese recognize any deviation from perfection, even if it is within the tolerance limits, results in increased costs.

VENDOR CERTIFICATION

Finally, most manufacturing plants have numerous machines supplied by various other manufacturing vendors. To ensure total quality, vendor certification and training should become a part of the quality improvement plan. However, work must be done in-house to clean up problems and learn the quality improvement process before beginning to ask vendors to implement it.

The new company-supplier relationship begins with the under-standing that you are partners in the same business. Both businesses' success is interdependent and must be approached that way. Any adversarial relationship must be eliminated.

Establishing vendor certification will require close coordination be-tween the engineering, manufacturing, and purchasing functions to determine the criteria. It also requires training for all these functions in the objectives and techniques of quality improvement.

The objective will be to establish long-term relationships that result in better quality from fewer suppliers. The relationships should be ones that result in:

1. Joint problem solving
2. Team product design
3. Sharing of technology
4. Sharing cost and production data
5. Quality that eliminates incoming inspections
6. Reduced total cost of raw materials
7. Continuous improvement to the relationship

Developing this vendor relationship will take time because trust and quality improvement will have to be established. The process should begin with a few critical vendors and gradually spread to all incom-ing material vendors.

Until these relationships are established, true world-class status cannot be achieved. Without world-class raw materials and world-class employees, it is impossible to produce world-class quality products. Also, world-class cannot happen when the people at the top think they have all the answers but have never walked in the employees' shoes or listened to them. Remember, we talked about destroying the brain line.

EXERCISE

List three Quality Improvement changes you will immediately implement for your team as a result of reading this chapter.

_____

_____

_____

SUMMARY

Yes, I have covered a lot of material in this chapter, but this may be one of the most important chapters in this book. Everything in business comes down to four things: 1) the quality of the product or service you deliver to the customer, 2) their perception of this product or service, 3) whether they share their positive experience with your organization with others (which drives more revenue and profits to your bottom line), or 4) whether they speak negatively of their experience with your organization privately to their network or publicly on social media (which can severely affect your ability to turn a profit).

I strongly recommend you and your team read this chapter over and over until quality is the benchmark of your organization from top management all the way down through every employee (especially those who actually do the work). After all, the frontline leader and their subordinates are the lifeblood and cash register of your business.

CHAPTER 20

MANAGING YOUR BUDDIES
AND SETTING DEADLINES

"It is all about quality of life and finding a happy
balance between work and friends and family."

— Philip Green

"You gotta make money off your friends because
your enemies won't give you any."

— Isaac's Saying

Now that you have all your deadlines down on paper or in your time
management device or calendar, I will give you some tips on how to
succeed in managing your buddies while keeping these friendships
alive and well. This knowledge and balance is crucial to your success!

MAKING MONEY WITH YOUR FRIENDS

As stated in my quote above, you have to make money off your
friends because your enemies won't give you any. See, it is okay to
hang with your buddies, go to a ballgame, go out to dinner, and
have a drink together, but when it comes to work and producing,

the pressure is on you as the leader to drive results. This means your buddies need to produce and you need to produce.

EXPLAINING THE RULES

If you work with your friends or buddies, you need to have a solid line of communication open with them so you can explain the rules. And rule number one is that business comes first because it is both your livelihoods. The next rule is that you need to succeed at becoming their leader, and you will need their help to be successful.

Once the rules are established and the line of communication is strong, both you and your subordinates need to know that confrontation is normal and natural. Any differences need to be discussed and addressed, and plans need to be put in place to eradicate the issues at hand. When issues arise, you and your friend, who may also be your subordinate, need to know that whatever happens at work will not interfere with your friendship. Likewise, whatever happens outside of work will not interfere with production goals and the work tasks at hand. It goes both ways. A special mature relationship is necessary from the beginning for this situation to be successful. Building this relationship is an art when you are the leader and have friends who may not understand business.

I suggest, if possible, you do not put yourself or your friend in this position. Remember: Never hire anyone you can't fire.

SETTING BOUNDARIES AT WORK

An example of setting boundaries at work with friends comes from my old friend Scott Maddox. Scott was a high school teacher and coach who went on to become a high school principal and earn his doctorate. Scott has always believed in hard work and accountability, and his high school always ranked in the top ten schools in Tennessee based on its test scores. Dr. Maddox often invites me to speak to his students. Just like I mentor frontline supervisors by walking around, I took a tour with Dr. Maddox, walking though the halls of his high school to speak to students and teachers and stick our heads into classrooms. This tour really told me a lot about his leadership and relationship-building skills. Every student and teacher we passed greeted him as "Mr. Maddox" or "Dr. Maddox." After years of friendship, I know Scott doesn't like excuses and is big on policies and procedures. He has also been a surrogate father to a lot of kids over the years; he reminds me of my dad, who was also a high school principal.

My point is Scott and I completely understood the boundaries he had in place in his school, and I treated him, his students, and his colleagues professionally while I visited. But behind closed doors, we could revert back to our friendship. Hence, when you and your subordinate/friend have the boundaries properly identified, harmony can and will happen, both at work and outside of the office. Behind closed doors, to me he is just Scott Maddox, so I can give him the middle finger with a smile on my face and say, "If I hear another person call you Mr. Maddox or Dr. Maddox, I will throw up!"

Holding your friends accountable won't work if they don't hold themselves accountable, no matter how hard you try to make it work.

SETTING DEADLINES

To help hold your friends or anyone you are leading accountable, it is always best to set deadlines. Deadlines will help everyone work together better because they will know what is expected of them and by when, and then they can strive to meet those deadlines.

When we want to achieve something, whether it's an individual, team, or company project, it is important to set deadlines. Why? Because deadlines spur actions. When directing a group of people, you need to head them in the same direction to achieve a common goal. To reach that goal, steps must be taken. To ensure everyone is working together, each step must be completed before you can move on to the next step, so each step needs a deadline. Each person may be working on an entirely different part of the process and need their own individual deadline. Each person's part or step in the process may be difficult or challenging so realistic deadlines need to be set for completion and for all the individuals' steps to come together so the goal can be reached on time.

As the leader, deadlines also give you the opportunity to coach the people not used to meeting deadlines and commitments. You are coaching them on how to become a part of something bigger than themselves.

Finally, setting deadlines cuts down on the confusion of who wants what. For example, Nellie was asked by her coach to send him a report "when you get a chance." Two days later, he was pressing Nellie, saying he needed the report yesterday! Makes you wonder how many days are in "when you get a chance." The best way to avoid this situation is to give the person a deadline. If you are the receiver of a task and your leader doesn't give you a deadline, then be sure to ask for one. If Nellie would have said, "What about tomorrow around noon?" and her coach had agreed, the confusion would have been eliminated. If you think you cannot meet the deadline given by your coach, ask for more time upfront, not when the deadline is upon you.

MAINTAINING FRIENDSHIP DESPITE TITLES

Bottom line, it is your goal and responsibility to create a culture of "productivity and attitude." You must create a culture of accountability so you can solve all challenges. And when you are disciplined enough to be friends outside of work and a leader during working hours, you can find a strong balance.

If your friend respects you, they will hold themselves accountable to the goal. Leading friends won't work if this foundation has not been set. After all, people will know you are friends, so they will be looking for inconsistencies in how you manage your friends versus everyone else. Keep this in mind and don't be weak.

EXERCISE

List one new way you will better manage your buddies.

_____

_____

_____

_____

_____

Now list two new deadlines you are setting for yourself or your team.

_____

_____

_____

_____

_____

_____

_____

_____

SUMMARY

Jobs come and go in today's marketplace. There is no such thing as job security, so I encourage you to do all you can to treasure your friendships and keep them as priorities in your life outside of work.

Never has anyone said on their deathbed that they should have worked longer hours, or that they had too many friends. Keep this in mind and you will succeed in achieving balance between managing your buddies and achieving your organizational goals. This balance is not easy to achieve, and even if you do it right, it still may not end well, so don't sacrifice your leadership for one or two people unless you are willing to do it for everyone.

When you explain the rules, set healthy, respectful boundaries with one another, and maintain your friendship despite your titles. Then you will succeed at managing your friends, while simultaneously achieving your Key Performance Indicators.

CHAPTER 21

CONDUCTING
ONE-ON-ONES

"90 minutes of your time can enhance the quality of your
subordinate's work for two weeks, or for some 80+ hours."

— Andy Grove

"Get to know your employee as a person;
then you can motivate them as an employee."

— Isaac's Saying

Now that you have a safe and healthy balance between your friendships and managing your buddies, in this chapter, I will share effective strategies for conducting one-on-one meetings so you not only
show you care about your employees' success, but you can also keep
the peace within your team. I will also introduce you to some role-
playing examples for one-on-ones that are straight from frontline
workers around North America. Reading and contemplating these
real-life situations and applying the wisdom communicated to your
management style will allow you to get the most out of your team
and better achieve your goals.

SAMPLE ONE-ON-ONE SITUATIONS

The following one-on-one examples illustrate how building a good relationship through regular one-on-ones with employees can help to boost morale, resolve problems when they arise, and lead to an overall healthier work culture.

Role-Play 1: Tardiness

Goal: To get James to consistently come to work on time.

Ike, James' manager, uses the following dialogue to work with James before he gets in trouble with the company's tardy policy. Ike knows from past experience that if he ignores James' tardiness problem, it will be more difficult to deal with later. Ike makes time for James in his daily scheduled one-on-ones to send a message to James of how much he is needed and how important he is to the team. The conversation may sound something like this:

Ike: James, you are a good worker and I'm pleased with your overall performance. However, I've noticed that you're often late. I depend upon you to be on time every day. It hurts the team when you are not here at startup. Is there anything preventing you from being on time that I can help you with?

(Ike knows to be silent while he waits for James' answer because if he speaks again before James does, his question will lose its power. He has just given James the power to change the narrative. Ike must keep James focused on the root cause of James' problem in order to improve his attendance.)

James: My youngest daughter doesn't want to get up in the morning, and I have to bring her to daycare before I come to work, so I end up running late when she doesn't move in the morning.

Ike: I understand. I used to have that problem with my kids when they were younger.

James: It's very frustrating. What did you do? I want to be on time for work.

(Ike now offers some suggestions of what worked with him to get his kids motivated to be ready to leave for school on time.)

James: Those are great ideas. I'll definitely try them.

Ike: Good. Let me know which one does the trick. You know I really do need you here on time. You're an integral part of the team.

James: I know. I appreciate that.

Ike: Also, you know from employee orientation what the company policy is about multiple tardies, and I would hate to have to discipline you or see you lose your job because your daughter won't get out of bed in the morning.

James: I understand. I appreciate you talking to me about it and the suggestions you gave me. I'll do my best to fix the problem right away.

The next day, James is only one minute late. Ike doesn't say anything about James' tardiness, hoping it's a sign of improvement since James has often been five to ten minutes late in the past.

The day after that and for the next two weeks, James is on time every day. Ike continues during that time to have daily one-on-ones with him. He does not harp on James' past tardiness or bring it up again until a few days after the above conversation, and only then because James tells him how his suggestions have helped him motivate his daughter to move on time.

Summary: This simple conversation became a win-win for James and Ike, as well as the company and even James' daughter, who no longer had to be scolded. It was easy for Ike to have this conversation with James because he had been building a relationship with James since he had been hired. Consequently, Ike was able to motivate James to improve his performance and to feel like a valued member of the team.

Role-Play 2: Coping with Frustration

Goal: To convince Lucy to share her frustrations in private with Greta.

Greta: You seem frustrated this morning Lucy; is there anything I can do?

Lucy: Yeah, you can make others do their job! I am tired of doing their job!

Greta: (using a slow, deliberate, and calm voice to settle Lucy down) What is upsetting you, Lucy? Please explain it to me so I can help you.

Lucy: People are not doing their jobs correctly, so I end up having to do their jobs!

Greta: Can you tell me where you think our process is bottle-necking?

Lucy, still frustrated, mentions a part of the process that involves a couple of coworkers.

Greta, knowing that she has to keep Lucy calm, states that she understand and continues by instructing Lucy not to display her frustrations in the department in front of her fellow employees because it hurts employee morale. She gently instructs Lucy on how she should conduct herself going forward in regards to this matter and others.

Lucy: I understand and would like to say I am sorry.

Greta: Good. I will look into the process to understand better where your frustrations are coming from. We can then discuss it further in our next one-on-one to see what improvements or changes we can make.

Lucy: Thanks

Greta: Thank you.

Summary: Greta knows her employees. She knows Lucy as an employee but also as a person. Greta knows she has to get Lucy to talk in a businesslike manner in order to have a constructive conversation with her. Greta also knows that if she doesn't stop the outburst and bad body language, it will affect her culture. She knows her people are looking to her to address the problem. Even though she solves both problems—Lucy's and the coworkers'—she cannot share what was said or done with them. That is why Greta has to see the problem in the process rather than simply take one employee's word for what the problem is. She also knows Lucy is a hard worker and self-starter, so she understands why Lucy gets upset when others are not keeping up their end of the deal. She finds ways to improve the process so everyone's job is easier to do and her employees can work together more smoothly.

Role-Play 3: Safety Requirements

Goal: For Eldo to get Nick to wear his safety glasses.

Eldo: How are you today, Nick?

Nick: I'm doing well. Thank you.

Eldo: Nick, we have to talk about why you are not wearing your safety glasses. Is there any reason you are not wearing them?

Nick: They keep fogging up.

Eldo: I understand. I gave you anti-fogging wipes. Are you using them?

Nick: No. I forgot.

Eldo: Okay. Please understand what our policy says about not wearing your glasses; you are putting me in a bad situation because you are a good person and a good worker. Policy calls for me to take the next step, which is a written warning. Do we need to go over the policy?

Nick: No, sir. I understand.

Eldo: Good. I just want to take care of you and make sure you are safe. I could never forgive myself if something happened to you while at work. Thanks for agreeing to wear them.

Nick: You are welcome.

Summary: Eldo knows Nick doesn't like change and likes to push the boundaries. Eldo is big on safety and will enforce the policy to the best of his ability. At the same time, Eldo wants his team to go home to their families as healthy as they were when they came to work. After noticing that Nick has worn his glasses for three consecutive days, he invites Nick back into his office to say thank you and tell Nick how much it means to him and to Nick's wellbeing that he's following safety procedures.

TAKING A PULSE ON MORALE

The best way to get a "pulse" on your organization's morale and take time to "inspect what you expect" is to conduct one-on-ones with your direct reports.

This process is best achieved when you go through the chain of command with no finger-pointing, but rather working as a team to come up with a plan and solve any issues. The farther you climb up the chain of command, the more you can see the challenges your organization faces. You must take a pulse at all levels to achieve the optimal results. One-on-ones are the best way to control this message and make sure everyone is on the same page relative to the vision, goal, plan, and process. Then you can get the desired results.

LISTENING TO MAKE THINGS BETTER

Before you can get everyone's buy-in to the common vision, you must be willing to meet all of your subordinates in their space, in their timing, with their mindset, and listen with your heart and soul. Your listening may make all the difference between their buy-in or rejection of the vision. Don't forget that rejection is an opportunity to teach.

Remember Teddy Roosevelt's quote, "No one cares how much you know until they know how much you care!" When you listen to others' concerns, you send a message to them that they are an important part of the team and you appreciate their efforts. When they experience this kind of caring from their leader, they will break through walls for you!

When your subordinates truly see how much you care, you will clean up the negative attitudes within your team. You will also clean up the stereotypes; you will create an environment where differences are irrelevant—white or black, male or female, Muslim or Hindu, it doesn't matter. You must teach your team how to work together as a team to support one another. Or at least respect them at work since you cannot control them once in society.

When you lead in this manner, you will achieve improved morale and higher productivity from everyone on your team.

For additional help and a quick guide, see Appendix B: Manager-Led *One-on-One* Meetings. I have provided an example for you there of how to hold the meeting and then a form you can use for your own one-on-one meetings.

1 | **GREET:** Break the Ice [Complete prior to meeting]

STEPS:
* Review previous one-on-one notes
* Note personal items that you can follow up on (i.e. son's baseball tournament, grandmother's health, etc.)

PURPOSE:
* Demonstrates that you care about the employee and their personal life
* Helps the employee feel comfortable with the meeting and most important, your relationship

2 | **EXPRESS:** Appreciation and Recognition [Complete prior to meeting]

STEPS:
* Note accomplishments since the past meeting—every accomplishment matters
* Accomplishments may be personal (i.e. maintaining a positive attitude), relational (i.e. helping a coworker), improved job performance (i.e. being to work on time), or goal related (i.e. meeting a deadline)

PURPOSE:
* Lets the employee feel valued
* Lets them know that you notice what they have contributed
* Creates motivation for continued success and effort

3 | **INVITE:** Feedback and Open Discussion [Take notes during meeting]

STEPS:
* Ask if there are any issues or items that are still pending from the last meeting that haven't been followed up with yet. What's gone well? What didn't go well?
* Ask if there are any issues on their mind to talk about today
* Ask them to provide feedback on you and your leadership style; communication or actions that may have caused mixed signals

PURPOSE:
* Transitions to a business conversation
* Reiterates that the employee's input is important
* Ensures items from the last meeting have been resolved
* Surfaces any unresolved issues before any new topics are brought up
* Clears the air of any misunderstandings

4 | **SHARE:** Updates on Company/Department Information [Complete prior to meeting]

STEPS:
* Consider all area of business that the employee should be updated on: policies, new products, customer reports, financial goals, marketing trends, etc.

PURPOSE:
* Prepares employee ahead of time for any change—give them time to accept and adjust
* Creates understanding to the purpose of the change and how it may impact their role
* Creates a space for them to share ideas and ask questions
* Allows employee to feel involved

5 | **DISCUSS:** Vision, Goals, Plans, Processes, and Results [Complete prior to meeting]

STEPS:
* Consider employee's role, determine what should be reviewed: Have goals or plans changed? Do processes need to change? Can the employee provide input?
* Ask questions to determine current state of mind and level of engagement
* Share results—especially those impacted by employee
* Share concerns
* Consider employee's performance and/or results; determine if further instruction should be given
* Determine if feedback or encouragement is required
* Ask employee for suggestions, input, and ideas

PURPOSE:
* Refreshes/reminds employee's focus
* Creates engagement
* Demonstrates your leadership to move things forward
* Discovers issues and concerns
* Involves employee in solutions

6 | **DECIDE:** Next Steps [Take notes during meeting]

STEPS:
* Based on discussion, articulate what the next steps are
* Give employee an opportunity to give suggestions
* Stay focused on results
* Come to a mutual agreement
* Always set a deadline or target date

PURPOSE:
* Creates collaboration and mutual understanding

7 | **DETERMINE:** Follow-up [Take notes during meeting]

STEPS:
* Together, determine when a good touch-point should be (most likely, before the next one-on-one)
* Be specific with follow-up by determining who, what when, and where

PURPOSE:
* Keeps situations on track and moving forward
* Creates accountability
* Determines roadblocks early

8 | **REFLECT:** Take Additional Notes [Complete immediately after meeting]

STEPS:
* Use this space to capture any additional items that you may want to follow-up on or remember for next month's meeting

PURPOSE:
* Retains pertinent information that wasn't written during meeting

DISCUSSION PLANNER

Manager-Led One-on-One Meetings

EMPLOYEE NAME: _____ DATE: _____

1   **GREET:** Break the Ice

Personal items to follow-up on

* _____

* _____

Personal items to follow-up on

* _____

* _____

2   **EXPRESS:** Appreciation and Recognition

* _____

* _____

* _____

3   **INVITE:** Updates and Feedback

Updates

* _____

* _____

* _____

Feedback:

* _____

* _____

* _____

4   **SHARE:** Department/Company-wide Information

* _____

* _____

* _____

* _____

5   **DISCUSS:** Vision, Goals, Plans, Processes, and Results

- _____
- _____
- _____
- _____
- _____

6   **DECIDE:** Next Steps

- _____
- _____
- _____
- _____
- _____

7   **DETERMINE:** Follow-up

Who:_____ What:_____

When:_____ Where:_____

Who:_____ What:_____

When:_____ Where:_____

Who:_____ What:_____

When:_____ Where:_____

8   **REFLECT:** Write Notes

_____

_____

_____

_____

_____

_____

_____

EXERCISE

List below the days and times each week that you implement a schedule for one-on-ones with your team.

SUMMARY

When you conduct one-on-ones with your team, they will perform at higher levels than if you skip this crucial management strategy. It is your responsibility to ensure you do this so they know exactly what your expectations are of them, both in production and attitude. Remember, there are two types of one-on-ones: scheduled and unscheduled.

Successful role-playing of one-on-one situations is one of the best training methods you can implement to cover all the possible situations you and your team may face on the job. Sometimes when you are managing your buddies, role-playing and one-on-ones may be a bit more difficult, but still very important.

As the leader of your team, you need to stay close to your subordinates so you can take a pulse on the organization's morale and take any and all appropriate actions when expectations are not being met.

Always remember that one-on-ones have to be based upon something. I recommend basing them on the organization's vision, the team's goal, and the worker's responsibility once the job has been well-defined.

CHAPTER 22

TRAINING NEW HIRES, INCREASING MORALE, REDUCING TURNOVER

"Morale is a state of mind. It is steadfastness and courage
and hope. It is confidence and zeal and loyalty.
It is élan, esprit de corps, and determination."

— George C. Marshall

"Turnover is the symptom, not the root cause,
of your organization's problems."

— Isaac's Saying

Now that you are effective in your one-on-one meetings or have a pulse on your team's morale, I will give you insight on how to boost morale and reduce turnover.

A human resource consultant has been quoted as saying the problem isn't when your employees "quit and leave" but when they "quit and stay," draining your company's resources, milking the clock, and not actually producing any real value to your team. Morale, turnover, and absenteeism are major issues faced by all management teams. Let's begin by looking at how to recognize their symptoms.

THREE FACTS ABOUT EMPLOYEE TURNOVER

Fact #1: One out of three new hires quits after only six months.

Fact #2: 33 percent of employees decide whether they will stay at a company long-term after the first week.

Fact #3: It can cost up to $10,000 to replace just one employee.

Do you have a plan to address these concerns?

ADDING UP THE LOSSES

Here is a turnover example from a recent *Huffington Post* article: You are a 150-person company with 11 percent annual turnover and you spend $25,000 per person on hiring. If you spend $10,000 each on turnover and development and lose $50,000 of productivity, your cost of turnover will be around $1.57 million. I have done the math over the years with the organizations I have worked with and found that replacing an employee costs an organization approximately $1,500 or more.

REDUCING TURNOVER

No matter how you slice it, turnover is a big deal for businesses, so finding solutions to retain employees cannot be taken lightly. If you're struggling with high turnover rates, you need a plan. Turnover is not a department, plant, or store problem; it's a corporate problem, meaning that businesses at the highest level need to help slow turnover through education and follow through on their companies' mission statements relative to their people.

The most important thing to remember about turnover is that, like a bad cough or sore throat, it's often a symptom of a problem, and not the whole problem itself. Nine times out of ten, high turnover rates are a sign of bad company culture. As a leader, it's your job to cultivate a positive culture that makes employees want to get up and come to work every morning. That's where any good turnover plan starts.

NEW HIRE TRAINING

After recruiting talent, the biggest next step is to develop that talent. I encourage every organization to develop a new hire training program. Most organizations are focused primarily on getting the product out or just filling a position with a warm body. Then management complains when a job is done poorly, which adds to turnover and morale problems, along with quality problems, poor order fill rates, and bad customer service. Most companies are not committed to training, yet continue to complain about turnover. Of those companies that are committed to training, very few do it well. I won't go into detail here, but I will give you a quick overview of what a training program should resemble. It boils down to three major steps:

1. Meet and Greet with Leadership.
Every new hire should meet with their leaders to start the relationship process and understand what each can expect from the other so they know how to support each other through good and rough times. The leader should send the message that they will visit the new employee daily to talk about their frustrations and then refocus on the new hire's commitment to the job.

2. Meet and Greet the Trainer.
Leadership should introduce the new hire to their trainer since the trainer will spend a significant amount of time with the new em-

ployee. The trainer will help the employee graduate from the training program by teaching them skills and evaluating how they learn (e.g., whether the person is an action learner, classroom learner, etc.) The most important skill the trainer must possess is people skills. The trainer must quickly build a relationship with the new employee that matches the leadership skills and relationship skills of their leader. The trainer is an extension of leadership, so every leader should clarify what they expect of their trainer and new hire.

3. Never Let the Trainer Be Pulled Away from the New Employee. Nothing is more important than training the new hire, except the building being on fire. Be committed and send the message that the new person is the most important person to you in the first few days and weeks. It's leadership's responsibility to see that this happens. Stop making excuses that we can't stay fully staffed when your heart is not in training and mentoring the people you lead and influence.

THINGS TO CONSIDER WHEN TRAINING NEW HIRES

Successful people focus on solutions while unsuccessful people focus on problems. Don't share your problems with the group. Most don't care, and 20 percent are glad you have them. Look for the good; look for the lesson in every problem, and focus on the solution. More people quit their supervisors than quit their jobs.

ATTITUDE IS EVERYTHING

It all comes down to attitude for all your employees. Once you understand that, you will learn how "easy" it is to lead. Here is an acronym I have used for years. It has served me and everyone I have shared it with:

E = ENTHUSIASM (It catches on like the common cold and nothing is achieved without it.)

A = ATTITUDE (It is important to stay positive and focused, no matter the situation.)

S = SOLUTIONS (Fix it. Fix it now. Don't ignore the problems. Stop all the damn meetings and fix it.)

Y = YOU (Get into you, as in "Hey, you over there" (your coworker), not "you" as in "yourself." It's not about you!)

EMBRACING THE MILLENNIAL MINDSET

I discussed Millennials in Chapter 7, but because they are now more than one-third of our workforce, I want to drive home the point of how important it is to embrace them.

From a leadership and mentoring standpoint, my goal with everyone I mentor is to connect our mindsets to drive success together; the goal is the same no matter the level of the organization or the generation. My goal is to connect us all together, no matter our age, generation, race, gender, etc.

I never try to change the younger generation, or the older generation for that matter. When I have my one-on-one with the person I am mentoring, I understand we may not have the same background. I haven't walked in their shoes, and I know people see the world differently. But I want to understand what they think, why they think the way they do, and most importantly, what motivates them.

My first priority is to build a relationship with them. After listening to them and analyzing what I hear, I try to add my wisdom to enhance their motivation and reasoning to help them become successful. Younger workers don't want older ways forced upon them. Instead, I build the relationship by incorporating my ideas with theirs while adding the business' etiquette and a respect for others into their ideas. There's an art and process in doing this. Remember, organization creates productivity; relationships create organization. Results depend on both. Trust equals access, and access equals information. The conversation is the "relationship," and it will always be that way.

FACTS ABOUT MILLENNIALS

1. Millennials make up the largest share of the workforce. More than 1 in 3 people employed are Millennials.

2. Millennials are ambitious job hoppers. On average, they change positions every 2-3 years, often to take what they see as a better or higher position.

As a business leader, you have to learn to work with the reality of these facts—and that reality gives you two options: do nothing and embrace the high costs of turnover, or adapt and create a culture that gives your workforce the incentive to stick around for the long haul.

Hopefully, you opt for the latter, and there are three ways you can achieve it as shared earlier in Chapter 7 in the article "Millennials Are Triangles" by my colleague Cary Tutelman.

INVESTING TIME TO GET TO KNOW YOUR EMPLOYEES

A good relationship with your employees always starts with communication and conversation. As stated above, most Millennials leave a job to take what they see as a step up for their career. That is because, despite repeated stereotypes, Millennials are highly ambitious. Often, it is the Baby Boomers who don't like change; they hold the belief that they actually once walked ten miles to and from work (both ways in the snow). The reality is Millennials have goals and visions for their lives, and they're more likely to take risks to achieve those goals than opt for stability like the Baby Boomers. Most Boomers want everything to go back to the horse-and-buggy era.

As an employer, understanding what's driving a Millennial worker will help you retain them before they make that move. This is why regular one-on-one meetings are so important; then you can incorporate your ideas with their ideas.

PROVIDE A PATH FOR ADVANCEMENT

Once you know what's driving the worker and what their goals are, show them how they can move up in your company and advance their career without leaving. Provide them with milestones and goals to achieve. Give them something to work toward.

When they're more focused on achieving something in your company, they'll be less focused on moving to another job. They want to work and learn from smart people, not bosses who criticize their generation for being different. They are less likely to take your shit the way the Boomers did.

THE MILLENNIAL MINDSET

Millennials' work habits differ from those of past generations. The biggest difference is Millennials focus more on actual work completed than time clocked, and they would prefer to spend their time working on something of quality than just busy work to fill up an eight-hour day.

Consider providing your employees with more flexibility in how, where, and when they work—but hold them accountable for their performance. Remember the goals, KPIs, etc.

WHAT YOUR ORGANIZATION MAY BE DOING WRONG

Before we can discuss ways to recruit committed people, I need to share with you the things you or your organization may be doing wrong that are pushing people away and causing them to quit and leave. Here is a list of the top ten ways to lose good employees:

1. Don't trust them to make good decisions.

2. Don't solicit their ideas and opinions or encourage involvement.

3. Don't provide flexibility on how and where they work.

4. Assume a paycheck is all the motivation they need.

5. Don't understand the differences in attitudes among today's multi-generational workforce.

6. Don't actively offer, encourage, and support professional growth opportunities.

7. Keep managers despite their incompetence in managing people and cultivating teamwork.

8. Be inflexible and unsystematic when it comes to work/life balance.

9. Don't recognize and reward employees' accomplishments, no matter how big or small.

10. Make them feel what they do is just a job.

Turnover is a symptom, not the root cause. But turnover can slowly decay your business like a termite eating away at your profits and customers. Here are some practices to help you improve your turnover:

1.   Determine the cost of turnover per person. Knowing that number will motivate you to reduce the cost.

2.   Find out what the root causes of turnover are; I am willing to bet leadership has a large role in those causes.

3.   Rethink using temp services—do they really care about you and your company, or are they just recycling people?

4.   Install an onboarding program and inspect it for consistency.

5.   Install a training program and inspect it for consistency.

6.   Install a trainer training program and inspect it for consistency.

7.   Create departmental training. Make it ongoing and intentional. You pay for the lack of training.

8.   Ensure all jobs are well defined with an SOP.

9.   Explain goals and KPIs by having productive one-on-ones. If you are not having one-on-ones, you are not connected to your workforce, and if you are not connected to your workforce, you are leaking profits—big profits—and losing people.

10. Train supervisors. Get the doer out of them. Failure to do so will result in lost profits, poor morale, turnover, poor quality, unhappy customers, etc. One supervisor trying to do everything rather than let their team is a recipe for disaster.

11. Create company policies and standards. They, in turn, will create your culture.

RECRUITING COMMITTED PEOPLE

You can improve retention and reduce turnover when you recruit committed people.

Most companies complain and talk about turnover, but very few have a plan with the passion to see it through to get their desired results. Mainly, this failing is because getting commitment from employees is not an item you sell or a service you provide; it's about relationships, understanding the individual, and integrating individuals into a system that is disciplined in people and what you produce or sell. It is not about getting the product out or selling at any cost! In other words, we don't see people as the assets we should, and we need to realize that to develop them takes time and money. But you will get a return in saving the millions you otherwise spend each year on turnover!

Below I've applied my five steps for Improving Profits Through People in relation to turnover:

- **Vision:** How do you see your company being successful by reducing turnover?

- **Goal:** Take your highest turnover department and set a goal to reduce it by a certain percentage. Tie that goal to the vision.

- **Plan:** What are you willing to accomplish, and what are you willing to plan to accomplish it?

- **Process:** Are your vision and goals working in the planned strategy?

- **Results:** Are you moving the needle of turnover reduction?

STAYING COMMITTED

Below are five detailed ways to help employees stay committed:

1. Hold Frontline Leadership Responsible

Frontline leadership should be held accountable to have a vested interest in turnover. They should also realize that many times they are the root cause of the turnover. Frontline leadership should be involved in building relationships and coaching their employees. Plus, adding turnover to their performance goals puts skin in the game. No one gets better if there are no consequences.

2. Training Programs

Review or implement a departmental training program. All training programs should report to the shop floor, not a training department within the company. The program should be based on job performance (unless the training department pays the price for a department that is underperforming). Hold a person accountable for a job that was very well taught. Some companies need to stop trying to run production and customer service departments from the top and let the leaders in the department do it. If the CEO, CFO, or COO is telling supervisors how to run their departments and picking their people for them, then when the numbers are not good, we should fire the CEO, CFO, or COO, not the supervisor or their employees.

3. Vision and Goal Training

Make sure everyone involved in reducing turnover is focused on the vision and the goal you want to achieve. Create SOPs and a plan to achieve the vision and the goal. Ensure everyone is very well trained on these principles.

4. Effective One-on-Ones

Constantly have one-on-ones to see where adjustments need to be made in the process with leadership, trainers, employees, new hires, and the onboarding process. One-on-ones will help get everyone involved in the culture change, and ensure you keep your foot on the gas.

5. Inspect What You Expect

After you teach the process, hold people accountable for what you expect them to accomplish. No exceptions!

ONBOARDING THE RIGHT WAY

Here are four ways to correctly onboard new hires to make it a smooth process.

1. Define the Process.

Start with the internal process. Define your onboarding program.

2. Create a Training Program for Leadership.

Create a standard SOP for this program and identify everyone who is involved.

3. Create a Training Program for Culture.

The people already in your company can add to turnover, so get them involved in a positive way, and hold them accountable.

4. Inspect What You Expect.

Inspect 1-3 above.

CLIENT CASE STUDY

Tyson Foods

Tyson Foods is one of the most recognized and successful food service companies in the world. It employs thousands of workers across the country.

I was hired to help management at a Tyson production plant to develop leadership skills and reduce employee turnover.

After assessing the root of the issues, we developed and implemented a training program that held leaders accountable for the turnover issues and provided the steps for reducing turnover by creating a better workplace culture, strengthening communication, and developing better protocols and processes for addressing employee concerns. We implemented this program over the course of two years.

The result was we reduced turnover by 30 percent and decreased absenteeism by 10 percent. These reductions resulted in a more productive workplace and cost savings that increased the overall bottom line.

EXERCISE

How can you boost morale?

_____

_____

_____

_____

_____

_____

_____

_____

_____

_____

How can you reduce turnover?

_____

_____

_____

_____

_____

_____

_____

_____

_____

_____

_____

SUMMARY

Employee turnover costs corporations millions and millions of dollars annually, which directly affects their ability to turn a profit. Often, people quit their leaders rather than their jobs. Hence, as the leader of your organization, it is important to have your leadership teams invest time in getting to know their subordinates, provide a path for them to achieve success, and give them the opportunity for career advancement. When your organization focuses on these simple, but often overlooked, strategies, a lot of time and money will be saved and harmony will exist within your organization.

CHAPTER 23

INSPECTING WHAT
YOU EXPECT

"Expectation is the root of all heartache."

— William Shakespeare

"Repetition is the mother of all learning."

— Isaac's Saying

In the last chapter, I shared with you proven and effective ways to boost morale and reduce turnover. In this chapter, I will help you know exactly what is happening in your organization, offer you strategies to correct issues, and in the process, put your team back on track to achieve your organizational vision and goals.

ASKING DAILY QUESTIONS

When I am coaching, mentoring, and developing leaders in organizations, I try to do so in a live session or via phone or email (but I prefer face-to-face so I can better analyze and prescribe the correct mentoring). I ask one or more questions to inspect what I expect after installing the Five Steps of Improving Profits Through People. Below are those questions and my reasons for asking them.

1. What Is Your Focus Today?

Each day brings a different challenge, but a leader's mindset has to be focused on people and processes. I need to know if there are motivation killers and then coach and mentor the leader through the process.

2. Where Are You?

There are so many moving pieces to implementing a system or new culture that you need to have an overall map of where you are at all times. I usually ask: Where are you on a scale of 1 to 10?

3. Have You Done Any Teaching?

I always ask this question because an opportunity will exist to teach or coach the process if they have not, or improve the process if they are teaching. Teaching has to be intentional and ongoing. Education in the workforce is vital to the department and company's success.

4. Are Your Team Members Well-Trained?

In order to have well-trained employees, every job has to be well-defined. If people have the physical and mental capabilities to do a job, they will do a good job.

5. Are You Inspecting What You Expect?

I ask this question to see if the leader expects anything, to test whether they are passionate about the visions and goals, and to determine if the vision and goals are becoming a reality. You can't inspect anything if you don't expect anything.

6. What Is Your Team's Morale?

Often, leaders think they are doing a good job with morale, but their workers will say differently. Set up one-on-ones to address the good, the bad, and the ugly, and then follow up.

7. What Are Your Challenges?

I usually ask leaders to keep a diary of what frustrates them during their day. Then I tell them to think through each frustration and put a plan together to address it. Also, they must ask themselves which of the five steps they and their organization need improvement in.

8. How Are You Handling Non-Performers?

Most leaders are unsure how to have a candid conversation with people who are not performing. Again, it goes back to where in the five steps did the coach misread or the team member just not understand. Work together to reteach and be patient, so long as you are getting the effort from the employee by using the task correction form (see Appendix A).

9. What Is Your Team's Overall Performance?

Assess your team's overall performance. Then put together a plan to improve it. How will you prevent poor performance from recurring? (Again, see the task correction form, Appendix A.)

10. What Is Your Department Training Program?

What methods are you using to inspect what you expect? A teacher must have an inventory of what to teach and a written or verbal test of the defined job or process that feeds into the vision and the goal.

I don't want to hear you tell me you showed an employee how it is done. I want to know how you taught and defined the job. Some leaders just cannot teach or coach. This process helps to ensure the job is being defined and taught properly.

For a quick cheat sheet of Daily Questions to ask yourself to ensure the job is being defined and taught properly, see Appendix C.

DON'T LET PROBLEMS RECUR

Not letting problems recur is a true measure of your success. How can you solve a problem in your process if you can't confirm what everyone is doing within the process?

Always teach:

- What you want
- When you want it
- How you want it
- Why you want it

See that it is done by inspecting what you expect. Your ability to follow this process with a mass group of followers is vital as you move up the corporate ladder.

TASK CORRECTION FORM

Remember to consult the task correction form previously referenced in this book. It can be found in Appendix A: Task Correction Form.

LOST PROFITS

World-class companies are world class for a reason: They believe in training, and they do it very well.

Many companies lose revenue due to inefficient leaders. This leads to inefficiencies in labor, which then leads to an unhappy workforce, high worker's comp, high turnover, and customer complaints—all of which cost the business thousands of dollars daily.

One main reason for lost profits is organizations treat the symptoms of their problems and not the root cause. The root cause almost always lies with the leadership of your business—especially those leaders closest to your customers and your workforce.

When dealing with efficiency issues, ask yourself:

- Has leadership been properly trained?
- Can they successfully apply their leadership training in accordance with your organization's philosophy?
- Do they have proper knowledge of the product and understand the process involved?

A poorly trained manager or supervisor can waste thousands of dollars per day. Remember, don't chase the symptoms; look for the root cause and address it.

EXERCISE

List three new inspection methods you plan on implementing for your team and add dates to each implementation.

_____

_____

_____

SUMMARY

I believe the absolutely best way to stay on top of things within your team is to "inspect what you expect," and the best way to do that is to ask daily questions, correcting areas and processes that don't meet your expectations, and consistently communicating your expectations to your team. When you do this on a regular basis, you will find your team will consistently achieve the plan that supports your vision and goals.

Additionally, by keeping your employees happy, you can stay union-free. That will give you the freedom to run your organization the way you and your organization desire to run it. Listen to your people.

CHAPTER 24

MANAGING CHANGE AND
AN INEFFECTIVE BOSS

"Outstanding leaders go out of their way to boost the self-esteem of their personnel. If people believe in themselves, it is amazing what they can accomplish."

— Sam Walton

"Give me a person with leadership skills and I will teach them the process."

— Isaac's Saying

In the last chapter, I offered proven strategies to inspect what you expect. Now, in my final chapter, I am going to offer you proven strategies for creating a great relationship with your boss and how to challenge your boss in the right way when necessary.

DON'T BE AN INEFFECTIVE BOSS

Ineffective bosses are everywhere. Be careful you don't become one.

Ineffective bosses make their subordinates less effective. They may have been effective employees, who outworked their coworkers and got promoted, but once in their new management role, they don't have the skills to teach, coach, or motivate their team to do their work properly. Most ineffective bosses will try to do the work themselves rather than delegate it. They will manage to get by using this type of management until they keep getting promoted to the point that they have too many subordinates and can't do all the jobs.

For an ineffective boss to improve, they must want to change. The difficult part of coaching an ineffective boss is when they are unwilling to change; then the challenge is to get them to see themselves and identify the imperfectness of their leadership ways. Also, remember it's hard to be a good boss; for one thing, people are always watching for how you are ineffective according to their own definitions of ineffective. To help manage your boss, try to have a face-to-face conversation to ask them what they need from you to be successful on the job, and walk through what success looks like in those areas. After reviewing, ask them that you be trusted in fulfilling and carrying out these duties, which will make their jobs much easier. Have a weekly meeting if possible to follow up what was agreed upon, and have patience because problems occur while building relationships.

MANAGING UP AND MANAGING CHANGE

Change is difficult for all of us, whether it's a new addition to the family, the loss of a loved one, family relocation, or changes in our jobs. In today's rapidly changing world of mergers and hostile takeovers, employees feel left out and helpless; coping with such changes can be quite stressful. Here are four tips to help you, as the leader, manage the change process to make it easier for everyone involved:

1. **Stay Focused:** Change can bring a lot of distractions, making it more important than ever to stay focused on

your job, the tasks at hand, and the changes within your department. Don't let your emotions cloud your business decisions. Give change a chance.

2. **Slow Down:** To stay ahead of the change, relax, think, ask questions, and get involved. Be a part of the change. There's nothing productive or effective about worrying over something you can't control. As the changes come, learn to adapt. By being involved, you can make the change easier for yourself and your team. Learning to adapt is one of the marks of a truly great leader.

3. **Stay Positive:** With any change, there's liable to be negative talk around the office. Don't participate. Negativity is poison, and you will always lose in the end. It's very important for you to stay positive, find the good, and be proactive about your situation.

4. **Get Your Team Involved:** It's true that many companies don't care about their workers' opinions or thoughts regarding change. Don't be one of those companies. Get your team involved in the change process by communicating the plan. At the end of the day, most of our fears are based on the unknown. If everyone is up to speed and aware of the situation, it makes it that much easier to stay positive, adapt, and continue down the path of success.

AVOIDING THE DIRECT APPROACH

More often than not, the direct approach for implementing change often does not work. The direct approach typically occurs when a manager forces change on their subordinates. People are resistant to change, especially in a work environment where they have been doing things the same way for years and years.

If the opportunity presents itself, a better approach is to get your people's buy-in by incorporating their ideas with yours and then executing the shared ideas until you achieve mutual satisfaction.

Whenever possible, let employees know what is going to happen before it happens. Explain that the change is intended to help build strategies and road maps to achieving greater success in their work. Most people fear the unknown. While some information may not be available at certain levels of the organizations, know what you can and can't communicate. Then communicate. Give honest feedback if you don't know the answer, and control the messages so you can control the morale.

IS YOUR BOSS A DOER?

We've all seen or heard of ineffective bosses and perhaps worked for one. Most ineffective bosses are not bad people; they are just doers. Yes, there are leaders with leadership skills who are ineffective bosses because of their boss mentality; they may be driven by status or power, so they behave negatively like a tyrant. However, we want to focus on the frontline leader who is an ineffective boss because of the effect they have on the company's bottom line and the customers.

Ineffective bosses are usually doers. A doer is someone who has done a job very well, was the last person standing through the turnover, has been with the company the longest, or was hired by another doer. Over the past ten years, due to cost savings and lack of education and training programs, most companies' leadership that is closest to the customer is filled with more doers than ever before.

Doers are promoted up through organizations, which leads to problems like turnover, bad culture, and eroding product quality. I don't believe labor is a company's highest cost; I believe inefficient labor is the highest cost. Doers don't plan; doers don't motivate. Doers cannot analyze their processes, and they minimize variables and increase inefficiencies.

Also, doers are usually yes men and women who depend upon their bosses to think for them. They may create project team meetings with data to help cover up their lack of leadership. The people who work for them (other doers) know this, and it leads to disrespect, which will go both ways and start eroding the relationship; after all, the doer boss and the doer workers know how to push each other's buttons because they were coworkers or came from the same group. Doers make ineffective bosses and shouldn't be in leadership roles. Doers are good at doing all or most of the jobs, but they continue to do them when they are promoted; they got promoted because they could do the job rather than because they had leadership skills. So they enter the leadership role without a plan. Disaster then starts immediately because they won't let their subordinates do their jobs, which leads to the morale eroding and lost profits through symptoms like customer complaints, high absenteeism, turnover, high workers' comp, etc.

Again, most companies chase the symptoms, not the root cause. For example, companies often tell me they have a turnover and absentee problem. I respond by saying turnover and absenteeism is a symptom, not the root cause. In most cases, those symptoms go back to the doer in the frontline supervision role. Training the frontline supervisor takes time and money, but most companies just want to get the product out to meet deadline, despite losing millions of dollars a month due to turnover and absenteeism! They only notice the problem when in a downturn and when profits are low, and even then, some companies still ignore it.

I consulted with a company that was losing twenty million dollars a year on turnover. To improve the turnover, I knew company training programs would need to be installed and the leaders' mindsets and habits would have to change. This company was filled with doers who had been promoted to middle and upper management. The training and mindset changes were a threat to them all. When that kind of pressure is on doers to change their way of thinking, doers usually stick together; because they are buddies, they won't let each other be exposed. If you are a leader and find yourself in this culture, you have two choices: join them or get the hell out before your career dies. Too many godfathers (meaning every boss in a high position takes care of each other, right or wrong) is a crime that robs the company and eventually the employees of meaningful and productive careers.

Your ineffective boss doesn't know how to build relationships. Doers put management of any given organization in a tough spot because they bring a great deal of knowledge and experience into the company, but they don't know how to lead. True leaders in the organization must recognize doers and enroll them into a leadership trainee program (an in-house training program for potential leaders). This program will help doers understand the importance of leadership. In most cases where I have coached and succeeded, the leader recognizes the doer needs coaching and mentoring to change their mindset, and the doer wants to change. However, it's difficult to change a doer without a demand from the leaders above the doer. A doer must have skin in the game to change and a passion to lead. If upper management is composed of doers or everyone is from the formal education system without work experience related to what you produce or the service you provide, the situation won't change.

Bottom line: Doers in management usually fail because they can't or won't delegate, and they also don't want to confront. To succeed as a leader, you need to do both.

TRANSFORMING FROM DOER TO LEADER

A few years ago, I was doing some one-on-one coaching with a young lady named Linda. Linda was one of the biggest doers I have ever met and one of my most difficult students, both emotionally and mentally. My friends and former students had told me that as a coach, I am direct and motivating. Linda, however, had a hard time dealing with me being direct. The more I pushed Linda to be a facilitator and not a worker, the more reasons she found not to change.

Linda and I talked about plans to reduce turnover, reduce waste, increase yield, and other items on her scorecard. In the past, other supervisors had found ways or excuses not to meet with me either because the process required too painful of a mindset change or they just enjoyed being doers. That led me to believe they all worked for the ultimate doer because their boss never sent them the message that they had no choice but to change if they wanted to improve as a leader. Linda, however, continued to meet with me—either she really wanted to change, or she just showed up to fight with me! Some days, I thought it was the latter. She always showed up on time for her sessions, and she always engaged in all of the teaching;

she was just mean! But perhaps she thought I was the mean one; in any case, she didn't run away. I never was an asshole to her. But I do tell people the truth. Some people think I am an asshole because no one has ever told them the truth before.

The other supervisors who had quit seeing me had ultimately given me the signal that it was time for me to exit because I couldn't help them if their bad doer bosses weren't going to support me. However, I stuck it out a little longer with Linda. One night (Linda worked third shift) we were discussing her KPIs and every task that wasn't performed well. Linda complained about the shortage of people in her department and the turnover problem she was having. I continued to tell her she had a vested interest in turnover and it was her fault (my being direct), but I could help her fix it. Too late! She was at her wits' end! Oh, the bad body language and the look she gave me. It would have killed the weak! But Linda didn't quit, and neither did I.

After a while, Linda and I built a working love-hate relationship. Each time we met, I would ask her if she was fully staffed. She would reply, "No." I would ask, "Why?" Doers don't like these questions because they have to strategize and come up with a plan, so her frustrations with me grew. One night, we were chatting about the movie *Ghost*. One of the characters in the movie is named Prospect Place Willy, so I started to call Linda "Fully Staffed Linda" because she needed to be fully staffed to reach her goals to be successful. By then, she understood that and really wanted to learn.

She wanted to be a leader, not a doer. Linda worked hard to change her mindset and habits. She had her challenges with people, coaching, and mentoring, but she didn't give up. I am no longer working with Linda, but we connect by phone, email, or text from time-to-time, and I am always excited to hear about the improvements she has made. We laugh about the times she hated me! She is putting in the hard work to erase years of being a doer. This change has not been easy for her and she's not perfect, but she never shorted me on effort. Being a leader is a gift, but effort is not a gift. She gave me all she had. I definitely think we made each other better! Her effort is what I am most proud of. Even though I told her what she didn't wanted to hear, she listened and made the transformation from being a doer to a facilitator. I am so proud of her for staying positive. When you are working with a group of doers, making the change is not easy.

EXERCISE

1. List a few management strategies you plan to implement to help you better manage your boss. (Make sure these strategies help you become a better leader than doer).

_____

_____

_____

2. Who is the most ineffective boss you ever had?

_____

_____

_____

3. List three reasons they earned that title.

_____

_____

_____

4. What did you want them to do that they didn't do?

_____

_____

_____

_____

_____

5. In your organization, who demonstrates the characteristics of an ineffective boss?

_____

_____

_____

_____

_____

6. Which characteristics of your ineffective boss do you possess?

_____

_____

_____

_____

_____

7. What is your plan to fix leadership issues in your organization?

_____

_____

_____

_____

_____

SUMMARY

Whether you have an ineffective boss or you are trying to prevent yourself from becoming the ineffective boss, remember to implement these four steps when managing change: stay focused, slow down, stay positive, and get your team involved. By doing so, you will be more effective at leading your team.

Additionally, do all you can to focus your efforts as the team leader on planning, facilitating, leading, and not "doing." When you become the leader and facilitator and you let your team be the doers, you will have a more engaged workforce and will also experience less turnover. If you lead in this manner, you will never have the "ineffective boss" label pinned on you. Instead, your team will respect you based on how you teach and trust them to do their job, let them solve their own problems, or help them when they need it.

A FINAL NOTE

ACHIEVING ORGANIZATIONAL
GOALS AND PROFITS

"Achieving conventional goals, such as profits and joy, with unconventional methods, such as investing energy instead of money."

— Jay Conrad Levinson

"Invest in your people and processes along with continuous education to achieve organizational goals."

— Isaac's Saying

Now that you have finished this book, what are you going to do? What actions are you going to take? What KPIs are you going to put in place? What silos are you going to address? What changes are you going to make in your organization to improve profits and reduce turnover? What relationships are you going to work on within your company to boost teamwork?

Before you put this book down and start on another, I suggest you order multiple copies of it for all of the managers and C-level executives in your organization. I encourage you to help everyone get on the same page so you can, indeed, change the momentum and get your organization moving in the right direction.

EXERCISE

Furthermore, my request to you is to get out a piece of paper, or use the exercise lines listed below to write out twenty actions you commit to taking to improve your organization and its profits within the next ninety days:

1.

2.

3.

4.

5.

6.

7.

8.

9.

10.

11.

12.

13.

14.

15.

16.

17.

18.

19.

20.

Perhaps one of these ten action items is to go back through this book and ensure you complete all the exercises at the end of each chapter.

Now that you have an implementation plan in place, let's summarize what you have learned by reading this book.

In *Improving Profits Through People*, you have learned how to assume nothing and teach everything. By doing so, your team is now better prepared and trained to achieve all the organizational goals you are charged with achieving. Furthermore, you have learned how to become the leader others *want* to follow. You have learned how to motivate your workforce to achieve Key Performance Indicators (KPIs). You have learned how to manage not only your friends or your bosses, but also all of your team to achieve common goals. Furthermore, you have learned how to build brand reputation and hire selectively to combat labor shortages. You have learned how to survive and reverse loss of profits, and how to nourish a safe work environment for your team so you can continuously keep employees motivated and earn profits. Most importantly, you have learned a proven, manufacturing, and service blueprint for "Leadership in a Changing World."

If I could summarize in one phrase this book and how exactly you can boost your profits, it would be: People respecting people. As a leader in your organization, it is your responsibility to level the playing field and lead with care. When your people feel you care, they will run through a brick wall to achieve organizational goals (and create better products and services for the customers, as a result).

So I challenge you to apply the wisdom, knowledge, experiences, skills, strategies, and techniques offered in this book to your life.

Then you will achieve what the subtitle of this book promises: "Boosting Your Organization's Bottom Line with a Results-Oriented Leadership Process." In doing so, you will literally improve profits through people, which is both the title and goal of this book. Bottom line: Teaching your employees how it's done is the key to improving profits through people. Remember, people are smart; they want to be a part of something special. The teaching philosophy in this book gives them the chance to be a part of something quite special.

Now that you have completed this book, please contact me to tell me what you liked and didn't like. What can I do to improve this book for the next edition? More importantly, tell me where you and your organization are in your journey, your organizational metrics, and your life. Perhaps we can talk by phone, or better yet, maybe you can book me to travel to your location to speak on some of this book's content to your organization. Then I can really dive into details and answer questions for you based on my and others' experiences.

I would like to offer you and your organization a no-obligation, complimentary 30-60 minute consultation by phone or in person to help you position your company for success, as well as to help you personally become a better leader. My cell phone number is 256-453-5577 and my email address is Isaac@SuccessPlusConsulting.com. Due to spam, I would prefer if you would text me directly instead of emailing me. Be sure to include your name and time zone so we can coordinate your complimentary session.

I hope this book can be a beginning for us and not an ending. I hope it will become the resource you have been searching for to make you a better person and leader, and be the catalyst you deserve to help you drive more profits to your organization, and more importantly, strengthen your relationship with your team.

I hope you have found what you are seeking in this book. I wish you and your organization all the success in the world. I wish you the courage to implement these techniques, strategies, and ideas to build a better you and a better organization.

To your success!

WHAT ABOUT ARTIFICIAL INTELLIGENCE AND GOING FORWARD?

ARTIFICIAL INTELLIGENCE (AI)

More and more company executives continue to ask me my opinion and thoughts about the impact Artificial Intelligence (AI)/robots will have on the manufacturing sector of our marketplace. That is a great question and a subject matter I have been studying for some time. Instead of allocating a whole chapter to this subject, I want to offer my judgment, both short and to the point, in this epilogue.

I believe robots will do a large percentage of manufacturing work in the future, but this technology will not completely eliminate people from the process. Many studies conclude that by the year 2035, there will be larger percentage of senior citizens in America because the Baby Boomers will have mostly retired, though some will continue to work.

As of this book's publication, a huge labor shortage exists all over the world, especially in aging economies like those of the United States and Japan. For these economies to remain economic powers, artificial intelligence/automation must become a huge part of their future. However, people and human capital will still play a major part in their success in creating an entirely different job market in some areas. Smart automation is the key to success, creating machines and robots that are so smart they can self-diagnose, which will make repairing them simple due to the lack of labor and labor mechanics. Can you remember when we used to have to update our computers? Now it's automatically done by the machine itself.

For an example, in the auto industry and some of the protein industries, labor is very intense, yet these are two of the most automated industries in the world. In these two industries, lots of employees are still needed to oversee this automation. Consequently, I don't believe robots will completely eliminate the human labor force. The benefits are that robots don't call in sick, and they don't sue their employers (a completely different subject for another day). I believe automation/robots and humans can and will coexist and work in conjunction with each other, and that situation will work out to be the norm. Contrary to popular belief, the problem today is not that younger people do not want to work, nor is receiving government aid anything new to the workforce or America. The reality is most companies were unprepared when the baby boomers left the workforce, so we have a much smaller pool of labor to draw from. The use of artificial intelligence will go a long way toward filling this gap in the workforce. I believe this change will be good for humans and will boost the profits of corporations worldwide. Change is good, and humans will work well with automation/robots because it will make our jobs easier, and in some cases, less dangerous.

The other concern I frequently hear is whether or not we should fear robots one day eliminating humans. That is a good ethical question, but one I will defer to the politicians and scientists since it is not my focus.

I am hopeful my thoughts on this subject will put your mind at ease and help you more confidently accept the many changes coming rather than resist them. Nothing grows without change. The challenge will be controlling the workplace between humans and machines by defining the human workplace in a particular business so a smooth transition exists between man and machine.

GOING FORWARD

From pandemics and downturns to political protests, we must acknowledge the variety of thinking in our society. Remember, society is "in your workforce." Keeping your team together at work may be more difficult for non-leaders and doers than those in leadership positions.

Achieving goals and communicating both your vision and your organization's vision are important for keeping people focused on their tasks. Perhaps now more than ever, conducting effective one-on-one meetings with the people in your workforce to get to know them better and understand their thoughts, beliefs, opinions, and biases is the key not only to keeping the peace within your organization, but keeping your team on track to achieve these visions and goals.

In our diverse world, it is your role to lead your diverse team through these challenges so we can all prosper and live in our world together peacefully!

APPENDICES

Appendix A
Task Correction Form

Appendix B
Manager-Led One-On-One Meetings

Appendix C
Daily Questions

TASK CORRECTION FORM

We teach because we care.

NAME: _____ DATE: _____

TASK DEFICIENCY: _____
_____
_____
_____
_____
_____

DATE(S) OF EDUCATION: **METHODS(S) OF EDUCATION:**

(1.) _____ (1.) _____

(2.) _____ (2.) _____

(3.) _____ (3.) _____

TEACHING OR COACHING TIME: HOURS_____ MINUTES_____

RESULTS: _____
_____
_____
_____
_____

DOES EMPLOYEE UNDERSTAND CORRECTION OF TASK? _____YES _____NO

NOTES: _____
_____
_____

_____ _____
EMPLOYEE SIGNATURE **COACH/TEACHER'S SIGNATURE**

NOTE: THIS IS NOT A LEGAL DOCUMENT FOR A REPRIMAND.
THIS DOCUMENT IS FOR GREATER CLARITY, AGREEMENT, AND
COMMITMENT ON HOW THE TASK SHOULD BE PERFORMED BY
DEFINING, TEACHING AND COACHING THE TASK.

www.successplusconsulting.com   /successplus   @successplus   844.467.7587   256.235.0710

MANAGER-LED
ONE-ON-ONE MEETINGS

1 | GREET: Break the Ice [Complete prior to meeting]

STEPS:	PURPOSE:
* Review previous one-on-one notes * Note personal items that you can follow up on (i.e. son's baseball tournament, grandmother's health, etc.)	* Demonstrates that you care about the employee and their personal life * Helps the employee feel comfortable with the meeting and most important, your relationship

2 | EXPRESS: Appreciation and Recognition [Complete prior to meeting]

STEPS:	PURPOSE:
* Note accomplishments since the past meeting—every accomplishment matters * Accomplishments may be personal (i.e. maintaining a positive attitude), relational (i.e. helping a coworker), improved job performance (i.e. being to work on time), or goal related (i.e. meeting a deadline)	* Lets the employee feel valued * Lets them know that you notice what they have contributed * Creates motivation for continued success and effort

3 | INVITE: Feedback and Open Discussion [Take notes during meeting]

STEPS:	PURPOSE:
* Ask if there are any issues or items that are still pending from the last meeting that haven't been followed up with yet. What's gone well? What didn't go well? * Ask if there are any issues on their mind to talk about today * Ask them to provide feedback on you and your leadership style; communication or actions that may have caused mixed signals	* Transitions to a business conversation * Reiterates that the employee's input is important * Ensures items from the last meeting have been resolved * Surfaces any unresolved issues before any new topics are brought up * Clears the air of any misunderstandings

4

SHARE: Updates on Company/Department Information [Complete prior to meeting]

STEPS:
* Consider all area of business that the employee should be updated on: policies, new products, customer reports, financial goals, marketing trends, etc.

PURPOSE:
* Prepares employee ahead of time for any change—give them time to accept and adjust
* Creates understanding to the purpose of the change and how it may impact their role
* Creates a space for them to share ideas and ask questions
* Allows employee to feel involved

5

DISCUSS: Vision, Goals, Plans, Processes, and Results [Complete prior to meeting]

STEPS:
* Consider employee's role, determine what should be reviewed: Have goals or plans changed? Do processes need to change? Can the employee provide input?
* Ask questions to determine current state of mind and level of engagement
* Share results—especially those impacted by employee
* Share concerns
* Consider employee's performance and/or results; determine if further instruction should be given
* Determine if feedback or encouragement is required
* Ask employee for suggestions, input, and ideas

PURPOSE:
* Refreshes/reminds employee's focus
* Creates engagement
* Demonstrates your leadership to move things forward
* Discovers issues and concerns
* Involves employee in solutions

6

DECIDE: Next Steps [Take notes during meeting]

STEPS:
* Based on discussion, articulate what the next steps are
* Give employee an opportunity to give suggestions
* Stay focused on results
* Come to a mutual agreement
* Always set a deadline or target date

PURPOSE:
* Creates collaboration and mutual understanding

7

DETERMINE: Follow-up [Take notes during meeting]

STEPS:
* Together, determine when a good touch-point should be (most likely, before the next one-on-one)
* Be specific with follow-up by determining who, what when, and where

PURPOSE:
* Keeps situations on track and moving forward
* Creates accountability
* Determines roadblocks early

8

REFLECT: Take Additional Notes [Complete immediately after meeting]

STEPS:
* Use this space to capture any additional items that you may want to follow-up on or remember for next month's meeting

PURPOSE:
* Retains pertinent information that wasn't written during meeting

---

DISCUSSION PLANNER
Manager-Led One-on-One Meetings

EMPLOYEE NAME: _____   DATE: _____

1   **GREET:** Break the Ice

Personal items to follow-up on
* _____

* _____

Personal items to follow-up on
* _____

* _____

2   **EXPRESS:** Appreciation and Recognition

* _____

* _____

* _____

3   **INVITE:** Updates and Feedback

Updates
* _____

* _____

* _____

Feedback:
* _____

* _____

* _____

4   **SHARE:** Department/Company-wide Information

* _____
* _____
* _____
* _____

5   **DISCUSS:** Vision, Goals, Plans, Processes, and Results

* _____
* _____
* _____
* _____
* _____

6   **DECIDE:** Next Steps

* _____
* _____
* _____
* _____
* _____

7   **DETERMINE:** Follow-up

Who:_____ What:_____
When:_____ Where:_____

Who:_____ What:_____
When:_____ Where:_____

Who:_____ What:_____
When:_____ Where:_____

8   **REFLECT:** Write Notes

DAILY QUESTIONS

INSPECT WHAT YOU EXPECT
Manager Daily Checklist

1 WHAT IS MY FOCUS TODAY?

2 HAVE I DONE ANY TEACHING OR COACHING TODAY?

3 ARE MY TEAM MEMBERS WELL TRAINED?

4 AT THE END OF THE DAY, DID I "INSPECT WHAT I EXPECT"?

5 HOW DO I HANDLE NON-PERFORMERS? REPEATED ONES?

6 WHAT IS MY DEPARTMENT'S TRAINING SCHEDULE?

7 WHERE AM I RELATIVE TO THE PROCESS I'M INSTALLING?

8 HOW MANY ONE-ON-ONES HAVE I SCHEDULED THIS MONTH AND PERFORMED?

9 WHAT'S MY TEAM'S MORALE?

10 WHAT ARE SOME OF MY CHALLENGES AND HOW AM I HANDLING THEM?

11 WAS MY TEAM'S OVERALL PERFORMANCE SUCCESSFUL THIS WEEK? TODAY?

ABOUT THE AUTHOR

ISAAC RUSSELL is an author, professional keynote speaker, mentor, nationally-recognized thought leader, and executive business coach. He is the founder and CEO of Success Plus, a leadership consulting firm established in 1993 that provides hands-on management training and coaching to companies in the industrial, manufacturing, customer service, and service industries all over the globe. Isaac has more than thirty combined years as a leader and business owner.

Isaac has helped some of America's most recognized brands—including Coca-Cola, Tyson Foods, and Johnsonville Foods—increase productivity, reduce turnover, boost profits, and create stronger relationships between leadership teams and their employees. He credits his success to the influence of the late George Howard, the man who pioneered the leadership of Alabama Industrial Development Training.

Isaac's book, *Improving Profits through People*, and his presentations help owners, managers, and supervisors learn how to increase their profits by investing in people.

One of Isaac's favorite sayings about himself is: "Southern born and Southern bred, and when I die, I will be Southern dead." He travels regularly throughout the world, but makes his home in Alabama.

ABOUT
SUCCESS PLUS CONSULTING

Success Plus is a leadership-consulting firm. It was founded in 1993 by Isaac Russell with the intent to provide hands-on management training, coaching, and mentoring to companies looking to build a better business.

Success Plus was created to provide companies with the insight and know-how to motivate people to do their jobs well. Success Plus strives to educate managers, supervisors, and upper management who have been deprived from the experience of working in the shoes of the employees they manage to improve the bottom line through effective management. This education process may range from improving employee turnover and diversity awareness training to one-on-one coaching, while specializing in day-to-day mentoring of supervisors, managers, and other upper management personnel.

Using a customized, personal, and hands-on approach (The Success Model), Isaac has had the pleasure of helping some of America's most recognized brands, such as Coca-Cola, Tyson Foods, and Johnsonville Foods, increase productivity, reduce turnover, and create stronger relationships between leadership teams and their employees.

The Success Model is a training philosophy based on the idea that those in a leadership role have a direct impact on company culture, which is the fundamental building block for success. Company culture affects everything from turnover rates to productivity, and it's the leader's job to cultivate a positive environment that promotes diversity, teamwork, and communication.

Therefore, the Success Model seeks to provide executives, managers, and supervisors with the characteristics and skills they need to get the job done, primarily: influence, self-awareness, insight, and empathy.

Although Isaac mostly develops his presentations based on the need of his clients, below is partial list of some of the speaking, coaching, and consulting subject matters Isaac presents on:

- Leadership in a Changing World
- Improving Profits Through People
- The Art of Accountability
- Leadership Coaching
- Improving Employee Retention
- Diversity Coaching
- One-on-One Mentoring
- Strategic Business and Leadership Planning
- Talent Development
- Life Coaching for Both Executives and Teens
- Leadership Training Programs
- Goal Setting

Isaac Russell credits the late George Howard's influence for the success he has accomplished in his work. George Howard pioneered the leadership of the Alabama Industrial Development Training programs and served as Director of AIDT from 1972 until his retirement in 1993. He always said "Attitude is everything," all the management of a given operation must be involved, and they must be instilled with the concept of industrial and service training of their people. Workers will do what is expected of them if they understand their jobs. If workers do not understand their jobs, management must assume the responsibility of educating them. If the education process does not materialize, then management must assume they are not doing their jobs. This assumption is one of the ingredients to the development of proper attitudes, and without the proper attitudes and motivations, you cannot have a smooth and productive operation.

For more information, visit the website below and then text Isaac with your name, time zone, and the best time to redeem a complimentary 30-60-minute, no-obligation consulting session by phone, Zoom, or in person (if geographically possible).

www.SuccessPlusConsulting.com
Isaac@SuccessPlusConsulting.com
Mobile: 256-453-5577
Office: 844-467-7587

Facebook: /successplusconsulting
Twitter: @spconsulting
LinkedIn: Isaac Russell
Google+: successplusconsulting